PIVOT POINT FUNDAMENTALS:
COSMETOLOGY
NAILS

ISBN 978-1-940593-51-7
ISBN 978-1-948482-50-9 (eBook)
ISBN 978-1-940593-56-2 (Coursebook set 101C-113C)

1st Edition, 1st Printing 2016
5th Printing, June 2022
Printed in China

Pivot Point International, Inc.
Global Headquarters
8725 West Higgins Road, Suite 700
Chicago, IL 60631 USA

847-866-0500
pivot-point.com

2

113ᶜ // NAILS
CONTENTS

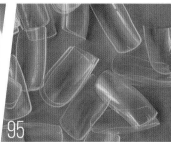

NAIL THEORY | 113^c.1

EXPLORE //

What do you consider to be the most important part of the nail?

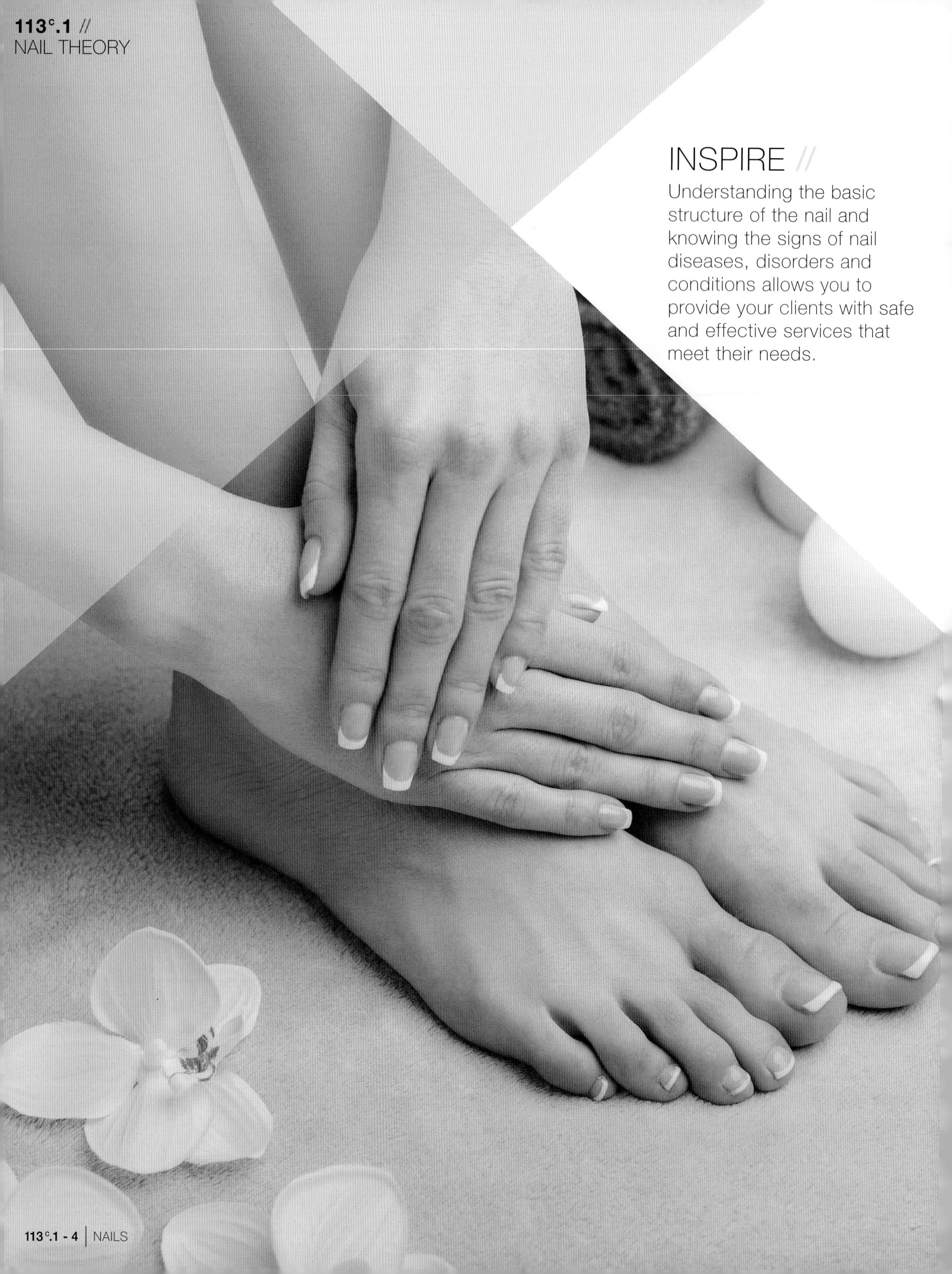

INSPIRE //

Understanding the basic structure of the nail and knowing the signs of nail diseases, disorders and conditions allows you to provide your clients with safe and effective services that meet their needs.

ACHIEVE //

Following this lesson on *Nail Theory*, you'll be able to:

» Identify the parts of the nail

» Explain the growth of the nail

» Recognize nail diseases that a salon professional may encounter during a nail and skin evaluation

» Identify nail disorders that a salon professional may encounter in the salon

» Give examples of nail conditions and available salon services that may help

FOCUS //

NAIL THEORY

Structure of the Nail

Growth of the Nail

Nail Diseases, Disorders and Conditions

113^c.1 | NAIL THEORY
STRUCTURE OF THE NAIL

Like the hair, the nail is an appendage of the skin. The technical name for the nail is onyx (ON-iks.) The study of the structure and growth of the nails is called onychology (on-ih-**KOL**-o-gee).

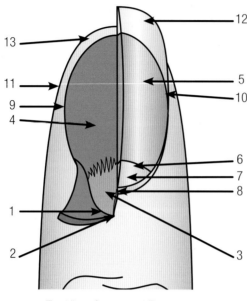

Top View, Cutaway of Finger

Side View,
Cross-Section of Finger

The best way to understand the structure of a nail is to look at a detailed diagram.

1. The **mantle** is the pocket-like structure that holds the root and matrix.

2. The **nail matrix** is the active tissue that generates cells, which harden as they move outward to form the nail plate.

3. The **nail root** is attached to the matrix at the base of the nail, under the skin and inside the mantle.

4. The **nail bed** is the area of the nail on which the nail body rests. Nerves and blood vessels found here supply nourishment. Specialized ligaments attach the nail bed to the bone.

5. The **nail plate** (nail body) is the visible nail area from the nail root to the free edge. Made of layers, no nerves or blood vessels can be found here.

6. The **lunula** is the half-moon shape at the base of the nail, which is the visible part of the matrix and appears lighter.

7. The **eponychium** (ep-o-**NIK**-ee-um) is the live tissue at the base of the nail; serves as a water-tight seal that protects matrix from infection.

8. The **cuticle** is the overlapping dead tissue that is loose and pliable around the nail.

9. The **nail grooves** are the tracks on either side of the nail that the nail moves on as it grows.

10. The **sidewalls** are the folds of skin on either side of the nail groove.

11. The **perionychium** (**PER**-i-o-nik-ee-um) is the living tissue that overlies the nail plate on the sides of the nail.

12. The **free edge** is the part of the nail that extends beyond the finger or toe and protects the tips of the fingers and toes.

13. The **hyponychium** (heye-poh-**NIK**-ee-um) is the living tissue underneath the free edge of the nail.

GROWTH OF THE NAIL

Like the hair, the nail is made of hard keratin. Although nail protein is much harder than the protein of hair, its growth is similar to the growth of hair.

Nail growth originates from the matrix, located in the mantle. The matrix contains lymph, blood vessels and nerves that create cells, which are pushed outward from the nail root. These cells keratinize (harden) and become fully hardened by the time they reach the eponychium. These hardened cells form the nail plate that curves on the sides and travels in the nail grooves. The rate of cell production in the matrix determines the thinness or thickness of the nail plate.

Nail growth facts:

» **Average fingernail growth rate is ⅛" (.3 cm) per month for adults.**

» Younger people's nails grow at a faster rate because general cell reproduction happens at a faster rate.

» Nail growth is faster in the summer than the winter.

» Under normal circumstances, it takes 4-6 months on average for a new fingernail to grow.

» As one ages, the growth of nails slows.

» Nail growth is affected by nutrition, health and/or disease.

» Middle fingers typically grow the fastest, while thumbs grow the slowest.

» Males' nails typically grow faster than females' nails.

» Toenails grow slower than fingernails but are harder and thicker than fingernails.

» It takes 12-18 months on average for a new toenail to grow.

Injuries to the nail can result in shape distortions or nail discoloration. Most nail injuries are minor and resulting distortions and/or discoloration are temporary. Permanent distortions can occur when:

» **A nail is lost due to trauma and, without the protection of the nail plate, the nail bed or matrix is injured.**

» **A nail is lost through disease or infection. The regrown nail, in these circumstances, is often distorted in shape.**

NAIL DISEASES, DISORDERS AND CONDITIONS

Any disease, disorder or condition of the nail is called an onychosis (on-i-**KO**-sis). The cause of the disease, disorder or condition is called its etiology (e-te-**OL**-o-je).

» **If a disease is present, refer client to a physician; no service should be performed.**

» **If a disorder is present, perform nail services with caution; client may want to consult with a physician for help and information.**

» **If a condition is present, perform nail services with modifications; nail should improve with correct techniques, products or improved nutrition.**

A study of onychosis considers four factors:

1. Identification of the disease, disorder or condition

2. **Etiology – The cause of the disease, disorder or condition**

» Systemic (meaning throughout the system) causes are internal, related to illness, nutrition or heredity

» Environmental causes include nail services or products (chemicals) that have adversely altered the skin or nail

» Disease-related causes, invasion of the skin or nail tissues by an agent like bacteria or fungi; these agents are contagious and spread by contact

3. Diagnosis—the identification of an onychosis through the symptoms and prognosis; the outlook for recovery

4. In-salon services:

» Products used and recommended for home care

» Techniques used and education for the client

SALON**CONNECTION**

A Change in Nails

As a salon professional,
clients will turn to you for advice
if they see a change in their nails.
You will recognize when it is something
you can help your client overcome or
when it would be more beneficial for them
to seek the help of a medical professional.

SKIN AND NAIL EXAMINATION

Begin every nail service by performing a skin and nail examination. Take a close look at the skin and nails and determine whether the client can receive the service they are requesting.

There are six signs of infection in the nail and skin:

1. **Pain**

2. **Swelling**

3. **Redness**

4. **Local fever**

5. **Throbbing**

6. **Pus**

A healthy nail is smooth, curved, and without hollows or wavy ridges. It is flexible, translucent and pinkish in color.

To perform an examination, start by washing your hands and having your client wash their hands. (When performing a pedicure, sanitize the client's feet first.) Then, turn the client's hands or feet over to observe the following:

» Temperature of skin

  » Cold may indicate poor circulation; heat may indicate infection

» Skin texture/feel

  » May indicate possible disease or disorder

» Inflammation/redness on skin or nails

  » May indicate possible disease or disorder

» Color/condition of nail bed

  » May identify visible injuries, disease and/or poor circulation

» Condition and length of free edge

  » May identify nail biting or dry, brittle nails

» Tenderness or stiff joints

  » May need to adjust massage techniques

» Shape and thickness of nail plate

  » May indicate possible disease or disorder

When a special condition exists, explain it to the client and suggest products and care techniques to help overcome the condition. **Certain nail irregularities must be referred to a physician for diagnosis or treatment, and no nail service performed until the condition is alleviated.** When in doubt, refer your client to a physician.

NAIL DISEASES

If any indicators of a nail disease are observed during the hand and nail examination, as a salon professional, you must refer your client to a physician.

NAIL DISEASES	IDENTIFIERS	CAUSE	DESCRIPTION	TREATMENT
Onychomycosis (o-ni-ko-mi-**KO**-sis) or **Tinea Unguium** (**TIN**-ee-ah **UN**-gwee-um)	**Ringworm of nail**	Fungus, disease-related, can result from a nail injury invaded by fungus	Nail becomes thick and discolors from black to brown or beige to white; can develop white scaly patches with yellow streaks under nail plate; deformed nail may fall off; must be diagnosed and treated by a physician	No service may be performed. Refer client to a physician.
Tinea (**TIN**-ee-ah) **Manus**	**Ringworm of hand**	Fungus, disease-related	Appears as rings containing tiny blisters, dark pink to reddish in color; can have dry flakes; can be confused with eczema or contact dermatitis; can spread to nails, scalp, feet or body; must be diagnosed and treated by a physician	No service may be performed. Refer client to a physician.
Tinea Pedis (**TIN**-ee-ah **PED**-is) or **"Athlete's Foot"**	**Ringworm of feet**	Fungus, disease-related; thrives in dark, moist conditions	Itching and peeling of the skin on feet; blisters containing colorless fluid form in groups or singly on sores and between toes, leaving sore or itchy skin on one or both feet; must be diagnosed and treated by a physician	No service may be performed. Refer client to a physician.
Paronychia (par-o-**NIK**-ee-a) or **Felon**	**Inflammation of skin around nail**	Bacterial infection, disease-related condition of tissue surrounding nail can occur if a hangnail gets infected; prolonged exposure of hands to water can create favorable conditions for paronychia	Red, swollen, sore, warm to touch, can lose the nail; must be diagnosed and treated by a physician; healing takes 4 weeks; nail may grow out deformed but can recover shape	No service may be performed. Refer client to a physician.

NAIL DISEASES	IDENTIFIERS	CAUSE	DESCRIPTION	TREATMENT
Onychoptosis (o-ni-kop-**TO**-sis) 	**Shedding or falling off of nails**	Disease- and injury-related	If the disease causing the problem is cured, the nail will regrow; may occur on only one or two nails; nail bed will be sensitive and should be protected while nail regrows	No service may be performed on affected nails. Refer client to a physician.
Onychia (o-**NIK**-ee-a) 	**Inflammation of nail matrix**	Bacterial infection, disease-related	Inflammation of the nail matrix, pus formation; red, swollen and tender; nail may stop growing, and plate may detach; nail may not grow back; if it does, it will probably be deformed; must be diagnosed and treated by a physician	No service may be performed. Refer client to a physician.
Onychatrophia (o-ni-ka-**TRO**-fee-a) 	**Atrophy of nail or wasting away of nail**	Injury or systemic disease	Nail shrinks in size and may separate from nail bed; if illness-related, may not improve if matrix is damaged; the nail may improve in 3 to 6 months	No service may be performed on affected nails. Refer client to a physician.
Onycholysis (o-ni-**KOL**-i-sis) 	**Loosening or separation of nail**	Internal disorder, infection or drug treatment; systemic, disease-related	Loosening of the nail plate starting at the free edge and progressing to the lunula; nail doesn't come off; stays attached at root area; must be diagnosed and treated by a physician	Do not touch. No service may be performed on affected nails. Refer client to a physician.

NAIL DISORDERS

If any indicators of a nail disorder are observed during the hand and nail examination, a service can be performed as long as no signs of infection are present. Some modifications to the service may be necessary.

NAIL DISORDERS	IDENTIFIERS	CAUSE	DESCRIPTION	TREATMENT
Blue Nails	**Appear bluish in color**	Systemic problems of heart, poor circulation or injury	"Blue" color in skin under nails; can be corrected if cause is eliminated; common in older people	Make client aware of problem and possible causes; suggest seeing a physician; perform manicure with caution, using light pressure.
Eggshell Nails	**Very thin, soft**	Hereditary or nervous condition	Thin nails; almost see-through, transparent	Protect with regular application of top coat, nail strengtheners or artificial nails as well as good dietary practices.
Corrugations (kor-u-**GA**-shuns)	**Horizontal wavy ridges across nail**	Injury, systemic conditions; uneven growth	Easily recognizable; if injury-related, it may grow out and disappear; systemic conditions may cause permanent ridges	Lightly buff to level the nail surface; apply a base coat or ridge filler to protect and even surface. Avoid over-buffing, since it is easy to thin the nail plate.
Kolionychia (kol-ioh-**NIK**-ee-uh) **or Spoon Nails**	**Nails with a concave shape**	Systemic or long-term illness; nerve disturbance	Unusual nail shapes; unlikely to disappear	File carefully; apply no pressure to nail plate; use polish to harden and protect nails.

NAIL DISORDERS	IDENTIFIERS	CAUSE	DESCRIPTION	TREATMENT
Furrows	**Indented vertical lines down nail plate**	Injury to matrix that causes cells to reproduce unevenly; can be nutrition-, injury- or illness-related; pushing too hard with pusher during nail service or exposure to harsh chemicals	Easily recognizable; may grow out; may be permanent	Lightly buff; apply base coat or ridge filler to protect and even out surface; perform nail service as usual.
Onychogryposis (o-ni-ko-**GRI**-po-sis) or **"Claw Nails"**	**Increased curvature of nails**	Systemic	Increased thickness and curving of the nail that may occur with age or injury to nail; most often occurring in the big toe; physicians may remove if severely deformed or difficult to keep clean	Look for signs of infection; clean well under free edge; file with emery board and keep nails short; only a podiatrist should trim.
Onychocryptosis (o-ni-ko-**KRIP**-to-sis)	**Ingrown nails**	Environmental or poor nail trimming practices; can become infected	If the nail grows into the edge of the nail groove cutting the skin, or becomes deeply embedded and/or infected, refer client to a physician who will remove the skin or portion of nail causing the problem; it may also occur on toes if shoes are too tight, or if the toenails are filed too deeply on sides	Thoroughly soften skin, trim nail straight across to prevent pressure on the nail groove. If infection is evident, do not perform service. Refer to a physician.
Melanonychia (mel-uh-nuh-**NIK**-ee-uh)	**A brown or black darkening of nail**	Increased production of melanin by melanocytes in nail matrix due to trauma, systemic disease or medications	Increased pigmentation results in darker bands that run the length of the nail; occurs more commonly in people with darker skin color	Make client aware of possible cause; perform nail service as usual.
Onychauxis (o-ni-**KOK**-sis) or **Hypertrophy**	**Thickening of nail plate or an abnormal outgrowth of nail**	Injury to nail or systemic	Easily recognizable; likely to disappear	Can be lightly buffed to even out the nail plate.

NAIL CONDITIONS

If any indicators of a nail condition are observed during the hand and nail examination, services can be performed. Nail conditions are generally minor irregularities and may require some modifications to the service.

NAIL CONDITIONS	IDENTIFIERS	CAUSE	DESCRIPTION	TREATMENT
Agnails or **Hangnails**	**Split cuticles; loose skin partially separated from cuticle**	Cuticle is overly dry and splits; environmental causes	Skin breaks at corners of nails; can be trimmed with cuticle nippers and may heal in 2-3 days; can be reoccurring	Trim only separated hangnail skin completely; moisturize and avoid massaging the area. Instruct the client to use cuticle oil daily. Hangnails may become infected if not properly treated.
Bruised Nails or **Splinter Hemorrhages**	**Dark purplish discoloration under nail**	Trauma to nail; environmental; blood trapped under nails or small capillaries hemorrhage	Discoloration under nail; normal nail growth will continue; bruised area will grow out with nail	No pressure on nail plate.
Leukonychia (loo-ko-**NIK**-ee-a)	**White spots appearing in nail**	Injury to nail, heredity, signs of systemic disorders or nutritional deficiency	A small separation from the nail bed; grows out with nail	Make client aware of possible cause; perform nail service as usual.
Pterygium (te-**RIJ**-ee-uhm)	**Living skin that becomes attached to nail plate either at eponychium (dorsal pterygium) or hyponychium (inverse pterygium)**	Severe injury to eponychium or hyponychium	Excess living skin that can remain attached to the nail plate and disrupt normal nail growth	No service may be performed on affected nails. If severe, refer the client to a physician.

NAIL CONDITIONS	IDENTIFIERS	CAUSE	DESCRIPTION	TREATMENT
Beau's Lines	**Indentations similar to horizontal corrugations that run across nails**	Growth at area under cuticle is interrupted by major injury or severe illness that has traumatized body for an extended period of time, such as uncontrolled diabetes or pneumonia	Nail returns to normal after trauma	Make client aware of possible cause; perform nail service as usual.
Onychophagy (o-ni-**KOF**-a-jee)	**Bitten nails**	Nervous habit, stress-related	Easily recognizable; if biting stops, the nails will regrow; may be sensitive to touch; nail plate will appear flat and may be deformed until an entire nail has regrown from the matrix; can completely recover	Perform nail service weekly, apply polish to nails.
Onychorrhexis (o-ni-ko-**REK**-sis)	**Split or brittle nails**	Injury, improper filing, harsh chemical contact	Easily recognizable; file with emery board carefully; may be a permanent condition	Soften nails well before trimming; offer moisturizing treatment; advise client to perform moisturizing treatments daily at home. Suggest wearing rubber gloves when hands are in water or chemicals.

Discoloration of the nail may indicate serious problems in the nail bed or nail plate. In general, all changes of color should be referred to a physician unless they can be removed by a cleansing agent like soap. Vitamin deficiencies, bacterial infections, fungal infestations, protein deficiencies, kidney or liver disorders, or reactions to medications can all cause discoloration. They should not be ignored. **The condition of the hands and nails will often indicate the overall health of the body.**

Bacterial vs. Fungal Infections

Nail infections—bacterial or fungal—can occur:

» On the nail plate

» In the nail plate

» Under the nail plate

Bacterial infections commonly occur either on the surface of the nail or underneath the nail, between the nail plate and the nail bed. They are most often seen as a green discoloration on the nail plate caused by the waste products of the bacteria. They are most commonly caused by improper nail preparation before applying artificial nails.	Fungal infections generally occur inside the nail plate and on the nail bed, causing it to swell and separate in layers. Early stages of nail fungus are indicated by a yellow-green spot that eventually becomes black. The area will look as though it is spreading toward the cuticle the larger it becomes.

You will see both types of infections in the salon setting. It is important to refer the client to a physician.

DISCOVER**MORE**

The condition of an individual's nails can provide information on their overall health. The discoloration of a nail may indicate a more serious systemic problem, such as a vitamin deficiency, protein deficiency, kidney or liver disorder or an adverse reaction to medication.

Diseases and infections are not spread simply by performing salon services; they are spread as a result of contact with an infected client and improper sanitation and disinfection procedures. It is critical to protect your clients and yourself by practicing proper infection control procedures.

Understanding the structure and growth of the nail and performing a thorough nail examination before a nail service will allow you to expand your services and inform your client of their best options.

LESSONS LEARNED

» The parts of the nail include: mantle, nail matrix, nail root, nail bed, nail plate, lunula, eponychium, cuticle, nail groves, sidewalls, perionychium, free edge and hyponychium.

» The nail is made up of keratin, like the hair, and has a similar growth.

» Common nail diseases a salon professional may observe in the salon include:

  » Onychomycosis or tinea unguium

  » Tinea manus

  » Tinea pedis or "athlete's foot"

  » Paronychia or felon

  » Onychoptosis

  » Onychia

  » Onychatrophia

  » Onycholysis

» Common nail disorders a salon professional may observe in the salon include:

  » Blue nails

  » Eggshell nails

» Corrugations

» Kolionychia or spoon nails

» Furrows

» Onychogryposis or "claw nails"

» Onychocryptosis

» Melanonychia

» Onychauxis or hypertrophy

» Common nail conditions, which may require some modification to nail services, include:

  » Agnails or hangnails

  » Bruised nails or splinter hemorrhages

  » Leukonychia

  » Pterygium

  » Beau's lines

  » Onychophagy

  » Onychorrhexis

What do you think are some of the most enjoyable things about getting a manicure or pedicure?

NATURAL NAILS

113^c.2

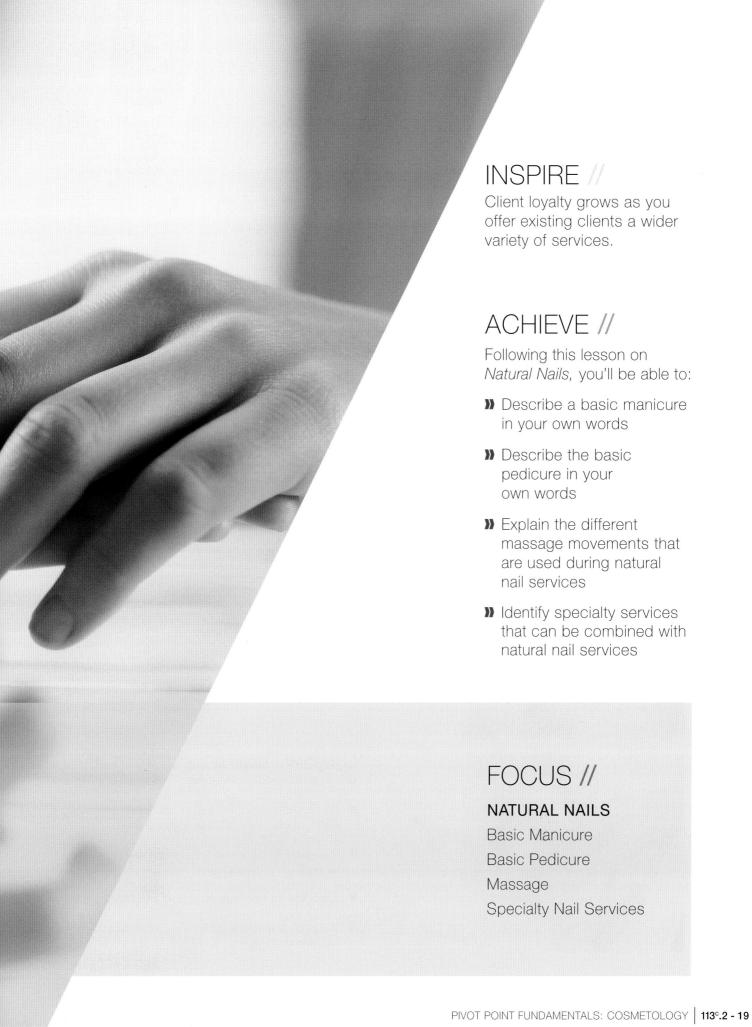

INSPIRE //

Client loyalty grows as you offer existing clients a wider variety of services.

ACHIEVE //

Following this lesson on *Natural Nails*, you'll be able to:

» Describe a basic manicure in your own words

» Describe the basic pedicure in your own words

» Explain the different massage movements that are used during natural nail services

» Identify specialty services that can be combined with natural nail services

FOCUS //

NATURAL NAILS

Basic Manicure

Basic Pedicure

Massage

Specialty Nail Services

113ᶜ.2 | NATURAL NAILS

BASIC MANICURE

A manicure is the cosmetic care of the hands and fingernails. The Latin word *manus* means hand, and *cura* means care. A basic manicure includes filing the nails, cuticle care, massage and polish. The basic manicure is the foundation for many types of manicures using different products such as paraffin, hand masks, exfoliants and anti-aging treatments.

	FILE	**File free edge:** » File from corner to center rather than sawing back and forth. » File all nails to same length and shape.
	CUTICLE CARE	**Push back cuticles:** » Apply cuticle remover cream to area using either a cotton-tipped orangewood stick, cotton swab or dropper. » Use light, quick circular movements in cuticle area. » Bevel nails by holding file at 45° angle to tip of nail and using an upward stroke to remove (smooths free edge after filing).
	MASSAGE	**Maintain contact once massage has begun:** » Lighten your touch and gently remove your hands at end of massage. » Provide an even tempo or rhythm and pressure to ensure a relaxing effect for the client.
	POLISH	**Apply polish to middle of nail, one side of nail, then other side of nail (middle-side-side):** » Hold finger between your index finger and thumb and pinch slightly to move sidewalls away from nail plate. » Place polish brush at middle of base of nail at an angle. » Brush toward free edge. Repeat on each side of nail plate. » Wrap polish around free edge if it extends past tip of finger to help prevent chipping.

FIVE BASIC NAIL SHAPES

The purpose of a nail service is to improve the appearance of the hands and, in particular, the nails. Part of beautifying the hands is filing to shape the nails. **There are five basic nail shapes: square, squoval, oval, round and pointed.** To offer clients the best shape and length for their nails:

» Use the shape of the cuticles as a guide

» Consider client's occupation, daily activities and hobbies

Square:

» Straight across at free edge and squared at corners

» Full width at tip of nail provides sturdiness

» Corners, though smooth, can break easily as they tend to catch on clothing and other surfaces

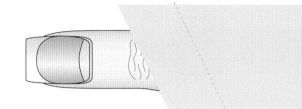

Squoval:

» Combination of square and oval shapes

» Straight across at free edge with slightly rounded corners

» Also known as "soft square" or "rounded square"

» Sturdy due to width at free edge

» Typically kept shorter

» Good choice for active clients

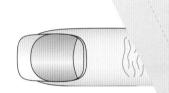

Oval:

» Tapered and rounded at tip

» Typically worn longer

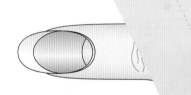

Round:

» Slightly tapered at tip; more "natural-looking"

» Typically worn shorter

» Most common shape for men

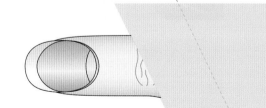

Pointed:

» Tapered to a slightly rounded tip

» Typically worn longer

» Tend to break more easily

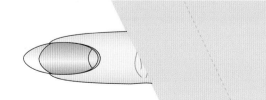

BASIC PEDICURE

Pedicuring is the cosmetic care of the feet and toenails. The Latin word *ped* means foot and *cura* means care. A basic pedicure includes trimming and shaping the nails, cuticle care, exfoliation, massage and polish.

	FILE	**File free edge:** » File from corner to center rather than sawing back and forth. » File all nails to same length and shape.
	CUTICLE CARE	**Push back cuticles:** » Apply cuticle remover cream to area using either a cotton-tipped orangewood stick, cotton swab or dropper. » Use light, quick circular movements in cuticle area.
	EXFOLIATE	**Apply sloughing lotion or foot scrub:** » Massage product onto skin to remove dead skin cells. » If needed, use foot file or paddle. Rinse each foot in footbath to remove sloughing lotion or scrub.
	MASSAGE	**Maintain contact once massage has begun:** » Lighten your touch and gently remove your hands at end of massage. » Provide an even tempo or rhythm and pressure to ensure a relaxing effect for client.
	POLISH	**Apply polish to middle of nail, one side of nail, then other side of nail (middle-side-side):** » Hold toe between your index finger and thumb and pinch slightly to move sidewalls away from nail plate. » Place polish brush at middle of base of nail at an angle. » Brush toward free edge. Repeat on each side of nail plate. » Wrap polish around free edge if it extends past tip of toe to help prevent chipping.

There are many different types of pedicures offered using extra products to pamper the feet, such as exfoliants, foot masks, fresh fruit and much more.

Pedicure Caution

Be aware of any conditions the client may have prior to the pedicure service—particularly, diabetes. It is extremely important not to create an opening in the skin of a client who is diabetic. You may also want to recommend that clients don't shave their legs within 24 hours of a pedicure. Shaving can create small micro-openings in the skin that may increase a client's potential for irritation.

MASSAGE

Massage is a systematic, therapeutic method of manipulating the body by rubbing, pinching, tapping, kneading or stroking with hands, fingers or an instrument. In ancient cultures, a massage was thought to have magical, therapeutic powers. Today, more people wonder if it's the mental state derived from the massage that helps a person feel better, or if massage has benefits beyond relaxation.

BENEFITS OF MASSAGE

As aging occurs, dehydration (loss of fluids) increases. Massage increases circulation to help remove waste from body cells at a more efficient rate. Increased circulation and renewed flexibility are two major benefits of massage. In addition to the physical benefits, massage is also emotionally soothing, since the human body responds well to touch that is safe, caring and confident.

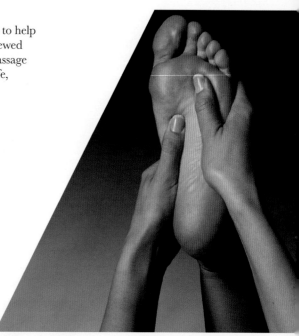

The many benefits of massage include:

» Increased circulation of blood supply to skin

» Tighter, firmer muscles

» Stimulation of glandular activities of skin

» Stronger muscle tissue

» Pain relief

» Softer, improved texture of skin

» Relief of emotional stress and body tension

The massage portion of a nail care service is generally considered the most relaxing and enjoyable part. Therefore, perfecting the various massage movements will ensure your clients come to you for their future nail care needs.

Important points to remember when performing massage movements are:

» Check for conditions listed on the right.

» Avoid massage that is too deep, aggressive or lengthy.

» Provide an even tempo or rhythm and pressure to ensure a relaxing effect for the client.

» Avoid removing the hands from the body once the massage has begun.

» Use feather-like movements to gently remove the hands at the end of the massage.

Massage Cautions
Avoid performing massage movements on clients with the following conditions:

» Skin conditions such as redness, swelling, pus, disease, bruises and/or broken or scraped skin

» Heart conditions/high blood pressure

» Stroke

» Pregnancy

Use caution when performing massage movements on clients with the following conditions:

» Prominent varicose veins

» Arthritis

FIVE BASIC MASSAGE TECHNIQUES

There are five basic massage movements. Each one performs a different function and delivers different results. Using different combinations of these movements delivers optimal results.

MOVEMENT	DESCRIPTION	EFFECT
EFFLEURAGE	» Light gliding strokes/circular movement » Performed with the pads of the fingertips or the palms of the hands » Often used to begin and end massage	» Soothing, relaxing
PETRISSAGE	» Light or heavy kneading, pinching and rolling of muscles » Performed by kneading the muscles between the thumb and fingers or by pressing the palm of the hand firmly over the muscles, then grasping and squeezing between the heel of the hand and the fingers	» Stimulates muscles, nerves and skin glands » Increases circulation of blood and lymph
FRICTION	» Circular or wringing movement with no gliding » Increases circulation » Performed with the fingertips or palms of the hands; rather than moving across the skin, the skin moves either across the muscle or the bone beneath it	» Stimulates and warms the muscles
TAPOTEMENT OR PERCUSSION	» Light tapping or slapping movement » Performed with the fingertips or partly flexed fingers » Invigorating movement that should not be used when the primary purpose is relaxation	» Increases blood circulation, stimulates nerves and promotes muscle contraction » Helps skin release carbon dioxide and waste material » Most stimulating massage movement
VIBRATION	» Shaking movement » Performed by shaking arms while fingertips or palms are touching the client » Only done for a short amount of time	» Very stimulating

SPECIALTY NAIL SERVICES

Do you know what makes a "spa" manicure or pedicure different from a basic service? Generally, spa manicures and pedicures are ordinary manicures and pedicures with some extras, known as "add-on" or specialty services. Although add-on services can turn a basic service into a spa service, they are more involved and require more products and skills. While clients benefit when you can offer them additional ways to enhance the appearance and general health of their hands and feet, you also benefit by increasing the cost of the service and thus, your profitability.

REFLEXOLOGY

Reflexology is a massage method that uses pressure on specific points of the hands, feet and sometimes the ears to relieve tension and influence certain body conditions. According to reflexologists—professionals who perform reflexology—distinct areas of the hands, feet and ears correspond with the body's internal organs.

Reflexology can be performed by itself or it can be added to the massage element of a manicure or pedicure. Check with your regulatory agency to learn whether reflexology can be practiced in your area.

AROMATHERAPY

Aromatherapy is the controlled use of essential oils that are highly fragranced for specific outcomes. Derived solely from plant matter, they are also known as aromatherapy oils. While the general public focuses largely on the pleasing scent of an essential oil, as a professional, the fragrance is secondary. Oils can be stimulating soothing, cleansing, calming or antiseptic to name a few uses.

Essential oils can be used in a room diffuser, or specific oils can be added to massage lotions/oils, masks, scrubs, paraffin or a hand and foot soak. When used in pure form (undiluted) these oils can irritate the skin and cause adverse reactions. Be sure to check each client's health history before using any essential oils. Use caution when using aromatherapy on any pregnant clients.

OIL	EFFECTS
Bergamot	Soothing; antiseptic
Chamomile	Soothing; healing
Eucalyptus	Stimulating; antiseptic
Geranium	Stimulating; antiseptic
Lavender	Soothing; antiseptic
Peppermint	Stimulating; antiseptic
Rosemary	Stimulating; antiseptic
Tea Tree	Stimulating; antiseptic

PARAFFIN TREATMENT

Paraffin is a type of wax that is frequently used for hand and foot services. Paraffin wax is heated, typically in a special heater, and then placed on the client's hands and feet. There are many different ways to apply paraffin; be guided by your instructor and your area's regulatory agency.

The paraffin absorbs and transfers heat to the area where it is applied. This helps soothe as well as moisturize the skin, leaving it soft and smooth. It's simple and quick. Clients love it because they can see and feel the results right away.

A paraffin service can be added to any natural nail service, prior to the nail polishing steps.

FRENCH MANICURE

A **French manicure**, or French polish, creates a natural-looking effect on the nail by covering the free edge, or tip, with white and then coating the entire nail with a sheer pink or beige color. The natural look of the nail is enhanced by emphasizing the white area of the nail. This area is often referred to as the nail's natural "smile line" because from the cosmetologist's point of view, the ends of the line curve up, and the nail appears to be smiling. White polish is applied to the nail to accentuate the tip and create a smooth smile line. The sheer polish enhances the healthy pink or beige color of the nail plate under which the nail bed is attached. There is a variety of sheer tinted polishes available for clients to choose from. Some manufacturers offer entire collections of colors appropriate for use on a French manicure.

NO-CHIP POLISH

No-chip polish, also referred to as gel polish, will typically last two weeks. No-chip polish uses an LED or UV light to cure each layer. It is applied similar to traditional polish with the main difference being that each coat has to cure under the light. No-chip polish is also removed differently than traditional polish. For removal, clients typically soak their nails in an acetone-based product designed to remove no-chip polish. It is highly recommended that you offer the removal as a service to your clients and that they do not attempt to chip the polish off on their own.

One of the biggest advantages for clients besides the long-lasting wear is that nails are immediately dry once they cure under the light. Clients can easily reach into a purse to get keys or put shoes on before leaving the salon. There are many product lines that offer thousands of available colors to meet clients' wants and needs.

NAIL DESIGN

Nail design, also known as nail art, is a great way to add a special touch to any nail service. Adding designs or accents to freshly-polished nails offers your clients a unique way to express themselves. Depending on the desired effect, nail design can be as simple as adding a rhinestone to a freshly-polished nail or as complex as three-dimensional designs sculpted with colored acrylic. Some clients may enjoy wearing nail designs year round. For other clients, nail design may be a service they choose for holidays or special occasions.

DISCOVER**MORE**

The average cost for a basic manicure is $20. Adding additional services such as a paraffin treatment increase the price. How much have you paid for a manicure? Did you have any additional services added to it? Why did you decide to add on the additional service(s)?

SAL**ONCONNECTION**

Value Add-Ons
A basic manicure or pedicure is an easy way to introduce your clients to all the services you can provide as a cosmetologist.

As your career progresses, you will continue to grow and learn about additional services you can offer your clients in the salon. The more you can learn and offer to your clients, the more they will trust you as a professional and will recommend you for more services.

LESSONS LEARNED

» A basic manicure includes filing the nails, cuticle care, massage and polish.

» A basic pedicure includes trimming and filing the nails, cuticle care, massage and polish.

» The different massage movements that are used during natural nail services include:

  » Effleurage – Light, relaxing, soothing
  » Petrissage – Kneading, pinching, rolling, stimulating
  » Friction – Circular, wringing, stimulating
  » Tapotement – Tapping or slapping; increases circulation; most stimulating
  » Vibration – Shaking, stimulating

» Specialty services or techniques that can be combined with natural nail services include:

  » Reflexology
  » Aromatherapy
  » Paraffin
  » French manicure
  » No-chip polish
  » Nail design

NATURAL NAIL
& PRODUCTS
ESSENTIALS

EXPLORE //

**Have you thought about what additional
services, other than hair services, you
will be able to offer your future clients?**

INSPIRE //

To offer the greatest variety of nail services to your clients, you will need a thorough knowledge of the products, tools or implements, supplies and equipment needed to perform natural nail services.

ACHIEVE //

Following this lesson on *Natural Nail Products and Essentials,* you'll be able to:

» Identify products, tools or implements, supplies and equipment used for natural nail services

» Describe the purpose they serve while performing natural nail services

FOCUS //

NATURAL NAIL PRODUCTS AND ESSENTIALS

Natural Nail Products

Natural Nail Essentials

Nail care, like hair design, is a science, a service and an art. Nail care can be an "extra" service you provide your client or it can be a creative specialty.

NATURAL NAIL PRODUCTS

To perform a professional nail service, you need a selection of products, tools and equipment. Natural nail products are produced by many different manufacturers, are disposable and must be frequently replaced. Regulating agencies require that Safety Data Sheets (SDS) are available for all products used in the salon.

PRODUCTS		DESCRIPTION	FUNCTION
	DISINFECTANT	Chemical product	Destroys or kills certain but not all bacteria and some viruses
	ANTISEPTIC	Liquid or foam-based product	Reduces microbes on the skin
	STYPTIC PRODUCT	Liquid or spray	Stops bleeding when applied
	POLISH REMOVER	Acetone or non-acetone	Dissolves polish
	CUTICLE REMOVER CREAM	Low-percent hydrogen peroxide, sodium or potassium hydroxide	Loosens dead skin
	NAIL BLEACH OR NAIL WHITENER	Lightener or high-percent hydrogen peroxide	Removes stains and whitens nails

PRODUCTS		DESCRIPTION	FUNCTION
	SOAKING SOLUTION	Soap used with warm water in finger bowl or pedicure basin	Softens skin, loosens dirt, aids in pushing back cuticle
	CUTICLE CREAM OR OIL	Moisturizer	Softens cuticle skin, moisturizes brittle nails
	LOTION OR MASSAGE CREAM/OIL	Lubricant	Softens skin and aids when providing massage
	NAIL PREPARATION SOLUTION	Dissolves oils on the nail plate; polish remover or alcohol can be used	Removes oil and product to help polish adhere to the nail plate; dehydrating product
	BASE COAT	Colorless polish that dries quickly; contains cellulose chemicals to create a tacky layer for polish to adhere to	Evens out nail plate, holds nail color to nail, prevents pigments from penetrating nail plate

Different types of products can be used to eliminate extra moisture from the nail plate. These dehydrating products include nail preparation solution, polish remover, alcohol and acrylic primer. Some manufacturers offer products that can perform more than one function, while others have separate products. Always follow manufacturer's instructions.

PRODUCTS		DESCRIPTION	FUNCTION
	TOP COAT OR SEALER	Colorless, clear polish that dries to a high shine; contains nitrocellulose which contributes to the shine	Protects colored polish from chipping, fading and peeling
	COLORED POLISH	Polish containing pigments to give color, enamel	Creates a colored effect
	SPEED DRY	Drying agent; spray, drops or polish applied over top coat	Aids in fast drying of polish; protects from stickiness
	NAIL STRENGTHENER (NAIL HARDENER)	Usually a colorless, clear polish applied prior to the base coat; may contain strengthening fibers, moisturizers or proteins	Prevents nails from splitting and peeling; provides moisture to dry, brittle nails
	EXFOLIANT	A granular scrub or sloughing lotion	Removes dead skin cells on the hands and feet

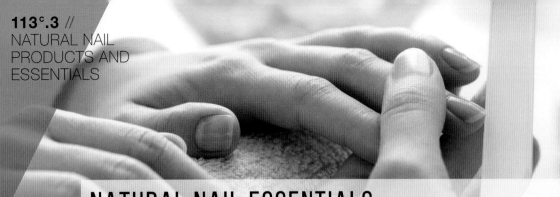

NATURAL NAIL ESSENTIALS

Nail service tools are the hand-held implements used to perform a service. They must be disinfected or discarded after every use. When determining whether an item can be disinfected or whether it needs to be thrown away, consider whether it is porous. For instance, an emery board is porous and therefore must be discarded after use, but a glass or metal file is not porous and can be disinfected.

TOOLS/IMPLEMENTS		DESCRIPTION	FUNCTION
	NAIL CLIPPERS	Two types – Fingernail (smaller) and toenail (larger); curved or s traight blades	Shorten nails
	NAIL FILE	Three types available » Disposable (Emery board) » Glass » Metal The higher number in grit the softer it is; 240 or higher should be used on fingernails to prevent damage.	Shortens and shapes nails
	CUTICLE PUSHER	Curved shape is designed to follow the natural curve of the nail	Loosens and pushes back cuticles
	CUTICLE NIPPERS	Two blades that pinch together to cut dead skin	Trim hangnails; check with your area's regulatory agency regarding usage

Since emery boards are not able to be disinfected, some salon professionals choose to offer the one used during the service to the client to keep.

TOOLS/IMPLEMENTS		DESCRIPTION	FUNCTION
	CURETTE	Spoon-shaped end	Removes debris from the nail margins/sidewalls; typically used on toenails
	NAIL RASP	File on the end designed to file in only one direction like a cheese grater	Smooths the edges of the nails in the grooves; typically used on toenails
	FOOT FILE (FOOT PADDLE)	Abrasive surface	Removes dry, flaky skin and smooths calluses
	NAIL BRUSH	Synthetic bristles	Cleans nails and removes debris before polishing
	BUFFER	Several types available: » 3-way buffer » Block buffer » Chamois buffer » Buffing blocks » Finishing buffers Follow regulatory guidelines on whether to dispose of or disinfect buffers.	Smooths surface of the nail

Credo Blade

This metal instrument holds a blade and is used for "cutting" calluses similar to how a potato peeler is used to remove the tough skin of a potato. The credo blade is prohibited by most regulatory agencies because it removes calluses by cutting the skin, which is typically only legally performed by a physician. Also, by removing the callus, the skin reacts by regenerating the skin cells rapidly to compensate for the loss—so most often, the callus comes back thicker. Calluses develop for a reason—to protect—and so it is not recommended to remove them, only to smooth and reduce them.

SUPPLIES		DESCRIPTION	FUNCTION
	COSMETIC SPATULA	Plastic, metal or wood	Removes product from jars; ensures infection control
	WOODEN PUSHER (ORANGEWOOD STICK)	Thin, round wooden stick with a flat end and sometimes a pointed end	Loosens and pushes back cuticles; applies cosmetics; cleans under free edge, removes polish from sidewalls
	COTTON OR LINT-FREE WIPES	Absorbent disposable material	Remove polish and oils from the nail plate; cotton can be wrapped around a wooden stick to create a softer edge; lint-free wipes are used when it's important no lint is left behind, also referred to as pledgets
	TOE SEPARATORS	Separate toes while polishing	Placed between toes before polish application
	PEDICURE SLIPPERS	Open-toed sandals worn instead of shoes while polish dries	Allow polish to dry
	TOWELS	Terry cloth washable or disposable paper towels	Dry hands and feet; can be folded into a cushion

NATURAL NAIL EQUIPMENT

Nail service equipment includes the furnishings and provisions necessary to provide a professional nail service.

EQUIPMENT		DESCRIPTION	FUNCTION
	MANICURE TABLE	Most have drawers for storing products, supplies and implements	Provides a flat, nonporous area to perform services on the hands
	TECHNICIAN CHAIR	Adjustable height, typically has wheels and the ability to swivel	Allows easy access to all tools and the client
	CLIENT CHAIR	Stationary chair; no wheels or swivel	Provides proper back support and comfort to client during nail service
	CLIENT CUSHION	Usually positioned on the manicure table or pedicure basin in front of the client	Used to rest client's arm or foot during service
	DISINFECTION CONTAINER	Large enough for complete immersion of implements	Holds disinfectant for disinfecting implements under infection control guidelines

EQUIPMENT		DESCRIPTION	FUNCTION
	COVERED CONTAINER	Space-saving container used to prevent cross contamination	Holds absorbent cotton, cotton swabs and other accessories
	LAMP	Attaches to the work area, uses a 40-watt bulb	Lights the area for close detail work
	FINGER BOWL	Large enough to immerse the fingernails	Serves as a container to soak client's fingernails
	PEDICURE STATION	Considered an "all-in-one" area designed specifically for pedicures	Provides a comfortable seat with arm rests, pedicure basin, foot rest and technician stool for pedicure services
	PEDICURE BASIN OR BATH	Large enough to immerse client's feet	Serves as a water container used to soak client's feet during a pedicure service

There are many different types of products available for nail services, knowing how to safely use them and following manufacturers' directions is your professional responsibility.

LESSONS LEARNED

The primary products used in natural nail services and their function include:

» Polish Remover – Dissolves polish

» Cuticle Remover Cream – Loosens dead skin

» Soaking Solution – Softens skin, loosens dirt, aids in pushing back cuticle

» Cuticle Cream or Oil – Softens cuticle skin, moisturizes brittle nails

» Lotion or Massage Oil – Softens skin, aids when providing massage

» Base Coat – Evens out nail plate, holds nail color to nail, prevents pigment from penetrating nail plate

» Colored Polish – Creates a colored effect

» Top Coat – Protects colored polish from chipping, fading and peeling

» Exfoliant – Removes dead skin cells on hands and feet

The primary tools and supplies used in natural nail services and their function include:

» Nail Clippers – Shorten nails

» Nail File – Shortens and shapes nails

» Cuticle Pusher – Loosens and pushes back cuticles

» Cuticle Nippers – Trim hangnails

» Foot File – Removes dry, flaky skin and smooths calluses

» Nail Brush – Cleans nails and removes debris before polishing

» Buffer – Smooths surface of the nail

The equipment needed to perform natural nail services includes:

» Manicure table, technician chair, client chair, client cushion, disinfection container, covered container, lamp, finger bowl, pedicure station and pedicure basin or bath

SALON**CONNECTION**

Clear the Area!

When you walk into a nail salon what's the first piece of equipment you notice? Some salons have elaborate pedicure areas with a nail drying station, which are very attractive to clients. Remember how important it is to keep your area clean and well organized with all of the products, supplies and tools you will need to perform the services you offer your clients.

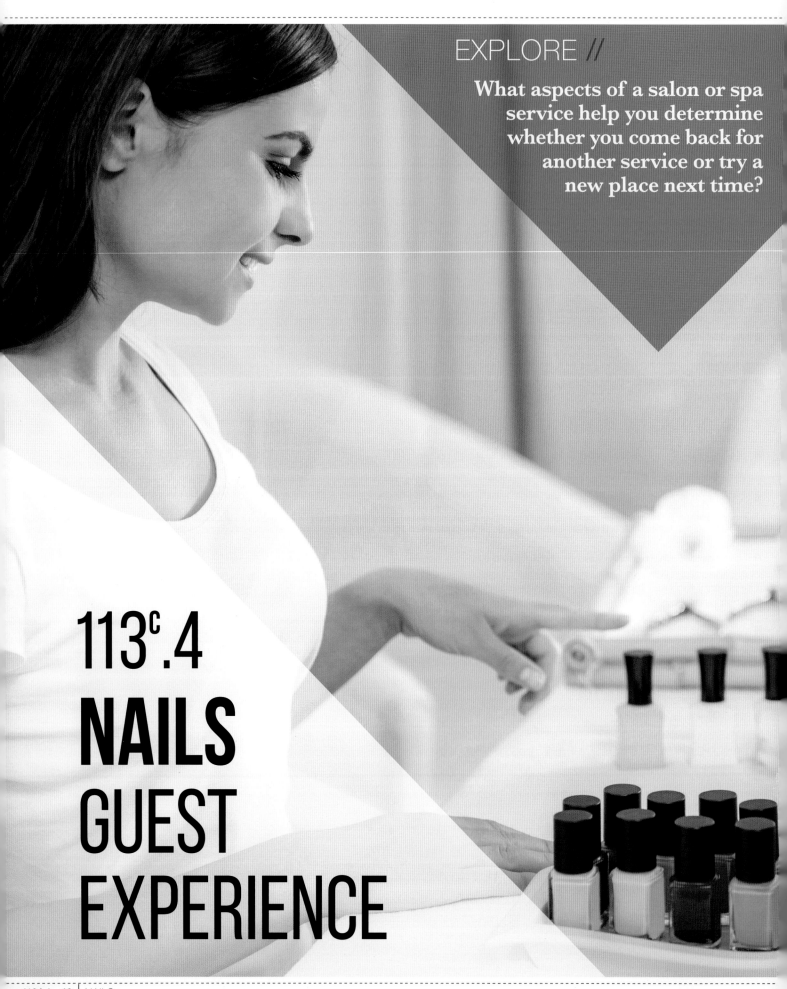

What aspects of a salon or spa service help you determine whether you come back for another service or try a new place next time?

113^c.4
NAILS
GUEST
EXPERIENCE

INSPIRE //

Providing outstanding guest experiences will ensure clients return to you for future nail services.

ACHIEVE //

Following this lesson on *Nails Guest Experience*, you'll be able to:

» Summarize the service essentials related to nail care

» Provide examples of infection control and safety guidelines for a nail service

FOCUS //

NAILS GUEST EXPERIENCE

Nail Service Essentials

Nail Service Infection Control and Safety

Salon professionals stand to gain by offering additional salon services to new and existing clients. Delivering professional and personalized nail services can help you establish rapport and develop a strong relationship with all of your clients. Satisfied clients will rebook and often refer their friends.

113ᶜ.4 | NAILS GUEST EXPERIENCE

NAIL SERVICE ESSENTIALS

The nail services guest experience is all about building rapport and trust with your client. As with all services, communicating with your client prior to and during the service will help you avoid misunderstandings and ensure predictable results. Listen to what the client tells you, but also see what their body language tells you. With nail services, making sure the client is comfortable throughout the service can be just as important as the final result of the service. The following guidelines will help you create a pleasant and lasting impression on your clients from the time you meet, through the completion of the service.

CONNECT

» Meet and greet the client with a firm handshake and a pleasant tone of voice.

» Communicate to build rapport and develop a relationship with the client.

CONSULT

» Ask questions to discover client wants and needs. Questions such as, "Do you have a special event coming up that brings you in for this particular nail service?" and "Do you like the length of your nails? What about the shape?" will help bring out what the client really wants and areas of concern the client might have.

» Ask questions about their lifestyle, such as "How much time do you have to spend on your nails?" If the client is leading a hectic lifestyle, you probably won't want to suggest nail services that would require regular maintenance.

» Ask questions about other services the client may desire, such as a paraffin treatment. Keep in mind that different services can complement one another. Explain the cost and maintenance associated with each service.

» Ask specific questions such as, "Would you like your polish to last longer?" or "Would you like a treatment to help with dry skin?" to uncover client expectations for their nail service.

» Analyze your client's skin and nails.

» Assess the facts and thoroughly think through your recommendations by visualizing the end result.

» Explain your recommended solutions, products and the price for today's service(s), as well as for future services.

» Gain feedback from your client and obtain consent before proceeding with the service.

CREATE

» Ensure client comfort throughout the service.

» Stay focused on delivering the nail service to the best of your ability.

» Explain to your client the products you are using throughout the service, and why.

» Allow the client to hold the product and test it to become familiar with the scent and feel.

» Produce a functional, predictable and pleasing result.

» Personalize the nail service, which may include a specific massage technique or aromatherapy with warm towels to add a signature touch.

» Remove any polish from the skin if polish was used.

» Teach the client how to perform at-home nail care maintenance.

COMPLETE

» Request specific feedback from your client. Ask questions and look for verbal and nonverbal cues to determine your client's level of satisfaction.

» Escort client to the retail area and show the products you used. Products may include cuticle oil and lotion or a nail file and nail strengthener. Recommend products to maintain the appearance and condition of your client's nails.

» Invite your client to make a purchase.

» Prebook – Suggest a future appointment time for your client's next visit.

» Offer sincere appreciation to your client for visiting the salon.

» Complete the client record for future visits; include recommended products.

Refer to lessons on the four Service Essentials for further guidelines.

COMMUNICATION GUIDELINES

The following chart offers common verbal cues clients give during a consultation and also suggestions for how to respond professionally and in a way that promotes trust and open communication.

CLIENT CUE	SALON PROFESSIONAL RESPONSE
"I've always wanted long nails."	"Do you mean you want your nails long now? Or, do you mean you have always wanted your natural nails to be long? If you want long nails now, I can add length to your nails with an acrylic overlay with tips."
"I just want a polish change."	"What type of polish do you have on, traditional or no-chip polish? Do you want your nails shortened and shaped also?"
"I only want natural polish."	"Are you saying you only want a clear coat on your nails? Or would you like a French polish, which features white at the tip and a light pink or beige color over the rest of the nail?" "Please point out some examples of natural polish that you like."
"I want my toenails shortened, but not too much."	"Where exactly would you like the edge of your nails to be? Would you like them right at the tip of your toes or a little past the tip of your toes?"
"Last time I had a manicure, my polish chipped the next day."	"I'm sorry you had that bad experience. Polish on natural fingernails tends to chip easily due to the natural oils in your skin, as well as how much you use your hands and for what types of activities. Have you ever tried a no-chip polish that can last up to two weeks? We can try that today and see if you are more satisfied with how long it lasts."

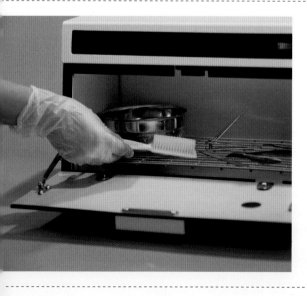

NAIL SERVICE INFECTION CONTROL AND SAFETY

It is your responsibility as a professional to protect your client by following infection control and safety guidelines with any and all services you provide.

Cleaning is a process of removing dirt and debris to aid in preventing the growth of microbes. Cleaning methods clean and reduce microbes on the surface, but do not kill microbes. Cleaning is performed prior to disinfection procedures.

Disinfection methods kill certain but not all microbes. Disinfectants are available in varied forms, including concentrate, liquid, spray or wipes that have EPA approval for use in the salon industry. Immersion and the use of disinfecting spray or wipes are common practices when it comes to disinfecting tools, multi-use supplies and equipment in the salon. Be sure to follow the manufacturer's directions for mixing disinfecting solutions and contact time, if applicable.

CLEANING AND DISINFECTION GUIDELINES

Keep in mind that only nonporous tools, supplies and equipment can be disinfected. All single-use items must be discarded after each use. Always follow your area's regulatory guidelines.

TOOLS, SUPPLIES AND EQUIPMENT	CLEANING GUIDELINES	DISINFECTION GUIDELINES
Metal Tools: » Nail Clippers » Metal Nail File » Cuticle Nippers » Cuticle Pusher » Curette » Nail Rasp	» Remove debris, using a brush. » Open hinged area to allow for thorough cleaning. » Preclean with soap and water.	» Immerse in an approved EPA-registered disinfectant solution, wipe or spray.
Manicure Station	» Remove all items and debris from table.	» Use an approved EPA-registered disinfectant solution, wipe or spray on all surfaces.
Pedicure Station	» Preclean basin/tub.	» Use an approved EPA-registered disinfectant solution, wipe or spray. See "Pedicure Basin Disinfection Guidelines" for more specific guidelines.

Store disinfected tools and multi-use supplies in a clean, dry, covered container or cabinet.

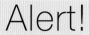 If tools, multi-use supplies or equipment have come in contact with blood or body fluids, the following disinfection procedures must take place:

 Use an approved EPA-registered hospital disinfectant according to manufacturer's directions and as required by your area's regulatory agency.

PEDICURE BASIN DISINFECTION GUIDELINES

To ensure the safety of your pedicure clients, it is especially important to sanitize and disinfect all pedicure basins properly. Following are guidelines to protect your clients:

AFTER EVERY CLIENT

1. Drain the water from pedicure basin or tub.

2. Scrub basin with soap and a disinfected scrub brush. Rinse with water to remove all visible residue.

3. Fill basin with water and the manufacturer's recommended amount of an approved EPA-registered disinfectant solution.

4. Allow the solution to circulate through the basin if it has jets. If not, allow the solution to stand for the manufacturer's recommended time.

5. Drain the water and rinse the basin.

6. Dry basin with a clean towel or single-use towel.

END OF THE DAY

1. Drain water from pedicure basin or tub.

2. Remove all removable parts, such as screens, filters, footplates and impellers. Scrub with a disinfected brush and soap and water. Be sure to scrub the areas behind the removable components.

3. Replace parts and fill basin with water and chelating detergent (cleanser designed for use in hard water). Allow the chelating detergent to circulate through the spa system for approximately 5-10 minutes or as directed by the manufacturer's instructions. Turn off the jets and let the solution soak for the remainder of the 10 minutes if it generates too much foam.

4. Drain the basin and rinse with water.

5. Fill basin with water and the manufacturer's recommended amount of an approved EPA-registered disinfectant solution.

6. Allow the solution to circulate through the basin if it has jets. If not, allow the solution to stand for the manufacturer's r ecommended time.

7. Drain the solution and rinse with water.

8. Dry the basin with a clean towel or single-use towel.

ONCE A WEEK

Follow the end-of-the-day guidelines; however, leave the disinfection solution in the basin overnight. In the morning, drain the solution and run clean water through the spa pedicure system.

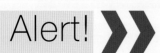 **A basin or tub that has come in contact with blood or body fluids must be disinfected using an approved EPA-registered hospital disinfectant according to manufacturer's guidelines and as outlined above.**

CARE AND SAFETY

Follow infection control procedures for personal care and client safety guidelines before and during the nail service to ensure your safety and the client's, while also contributing to the salon care.

Personal Care	Client Care Prior to the Service	Client Care During the Service	Salon Care
» Check that your personal standards of health and hygiene minimize the spread of infection.	» Check the skin and nails for any diseases or disorders. If any are evident, refer the client to a physician and do not proceed with the service.	» If you cut the client or yourself, immediately apply first-aid procedures. If wound is deep, seek emergency medical attention.	» Follow health and safety guidelines, including cleaning and disinfecting procedures. » Ensure equipment, including the chair, is clean and disinfected.
» Wash hands and dry thoroughly with a single-use towel.	» Protect the client's skin and clothing from water with a freshly laundered towel, if necessary.	» Be aware of any sensitivity while massaging.	» Promote a professional image by ensuring your workstation is clean and tidy throughout the service.
» Disinfect workstation.	» Handle tools with care to ensure your safety and that of your client.	» Work carefully around nonremovable jewelry/piercings.	» Disinfect all tools after each use. Always use disinfected tools for each client. » Ensure electrical cords are properly positioned to avoid accidental falls.
» Clean and disinfect tools appropriately.	» If any tools are dropped on the floor be sure to pick them up, then clean and disinfect.	» Be aware of nonverbal cues the client may be conveying.	» Ensure electrical equipment, plugs and cables are in good condition, and remember to turn off after use.
» Wear single-use gloves as required.		» Store soiled towels in a dry, covered receptacle until laundered.	» Sweep or vacuum and dispose of nail clippings at the end of the service.
» Minimize fatigue by maintaining good posture during the service.		» Update the client record, noting nail or skin conditions and services provided.	» Report malfunctioning furniture/equipment to manager.
» Refer to your area's regulatory agency for proper mixing/handling of disinfection solutions.			» Clean/mop water spillage from floor to avoid accidental falls.

DISCOVER**MORE**

Regulatory Agency – It's the Law!

Client protection is up to you! Disinfection of pedicure tubs and basins is always a hot topic; are you doing enough? Remember to follow your area's regulatory agency and manufacturer's recommendations when it comes to the proper cleaning and disinfection of pedicure tubs/basins. Join an association to keep up to date on changes and what disinfection products are available to protect your clients.

SALON**CONNECTION**

Make It Easy

Help your clients keep their freshly polished nails smudge-free. Once you have gained your client's trust, ask if they would prefer to take a moment prior to the polish application to pay or take out their keys. Explain that you would like to make things easier for them after the service. They will appreciate the thought and convenience.

LESSONS LEARNED

» The service essentials related to nail services can be summarized as follows:

» Connect – Meet and greet client to build rapport.

» Consult – Ask questions to discover client needs; analyze skin and nails; assess the facts to make recommendations; explain recommended solutions and gain feedback for consent to move forward.

» Create – Ensure client safety and comfort; stay focused to deliver the best service; teach and explain the products to your client; teach the client at-home care and maintenance.

» Complete – Request specific feedback; show products used; suggest future appointment times; complete client record.

» Infection control and safety guidelines must be followed throughout a nail service to ensure your safety and the safety of the client and the salon. Disinfectants are available in varied forms, including concentrate, liquid, spray or wipes that have EPA approval for use in the salon industry. Be guided by your area's regulatory agency for proper cleaning and disinfection guidelines.

By following the four Service Essentials and following proper infection control and safety guidelines, you will be able to create a pleasant salon experience and build a loyal clientele.

113ᶜ.5
NATURAL NAIL SERVICE

EXPLORE //

Have you ever received a nail service that didn't meet your expectations?

INSPIRE //

Following natural nail service procedures will help you provide a smooth and organized client experience, which will meet each client's expectations and generate referrals for you.

ACHIEVE //

Following this lesson on *Natural Nail Service*, you'll be able to:

» Provide examples of guidelines to follow when performing a natural nail service

» Describe the three areas of a natural nail service

FOCUS //

NATURAL NAIL SERVICE

Natural Nail Client Guidelines

Natural Nail Service Overview

Natural Nail Rubrics

113^c.5 | NATURAL NAIL SERVICE

Knowledge of the products, tools and services available for natural nails allows you to add these services to your salon repertoire. Combine that with your knowledge of guest relations and lots of practice, and you'll be able to provide professional natural nail services that will leave your clients with a lasting impression that goes beyond being pleased with the final result.

NATURAL NAIL CLIENT GUIDELINES

Now that you have a thorough understanding of natural nail service, you're ready to begin applying your knowledge by performing safe and comfortable services with professional results.

These guidelines will help ensure your client's comfort and safety during a nail service.

	FILE	**File the free edge:** » Consult with client on desired shape and length. » To remove length, trim nails with clippers before filing. » Check for client approval after filing and shaping.
	CUTICLE CARE	**Push back cuticles:** » Use light, quick circular movements in cuticle area. » Check for client comfort while pushing cuticles back.
	EXFOLIATE	**Exfoliate using a product or implement:** » Avoid being aggressive with any exfoliation method. » Check client's comfort; sometimes this can be very uncomfortable for the client. » When using a granular scrub, don't apply too much pressure.
	MASSAGE	**Maintain contact once massage has begun:** » Throughout massage, check that pressure is comfortable for client. » Avoid too much pressure directly over bones. » Avoid using too heavily scented lotions or creams. » Provide an even rhythm and pressure to ensure a relaxing effect for client. » Lighten your touch and gently remove your hands at end of a massage.
	POLISH	**Apply polish to nail plate (middle-side-side):** » Hold finger or toe between your index finger and thumb and pinch slightly to move the sidewalls away from nail plate. » Polish a couple of nails and check that client likes color. » Wrap the polish around the free edge if it extends past the tip of the finger or toe to help prevent chipping.

NATURAL NAIL SERVICE OVERVIEW

The Natural Nail Service Overview identifies the three areas of every natural nail service.

» The Natural Nail Preparation provides a brief overview of the steps to follow *before* you actually begin the nail service.

» The Natural Nail Service Procedure provides an overview of the steps that you'll use *during* the nail service to ensure predictable results.

» The Natural Nail Service Completion provides an overview of the steps to follow *after* performing the nail service to ensure guest satisfaction.

Service Essentials: The Four Cs

The natural nail procedures include attention to the four Cs.

1. **CONNECT**
   » Greet the client and communicate.

   » Build rapport and develop a relationship.

2. **CONSULT**
   » Ask questions to discover client's needs and wants.

   » Analyze the hands and nails and check for any contraindications.

   » Gain approval before proceeding with the service.

3. **CREATE**
   » Ensure client protection and comfort.

   » Create predictable natural nail service results.

4. **COMPLETE**
   » Share appropriate follow-up care.

NATURAL NAIL SERVICE OVERVIEW

NATURAL NAIL SERVICE PREPARATION	» Clean and disinfect workstation. » Arrange disinfected tools, supplies and equipment. » Wash your hands. » Ask client to remove and store jewelry (rings, bracelets, watches, etc.) » Sanitize client's hands or feet, and perform a visual analysis of skin and nails. » Consult with client about the desired shape and/or length of the nails.
NATURAL NAIL SERVICE PROCEDURE	» Perform natural nail service procedures to achieve desired results: 1. **File** and shape the nails on the first hand/foot; soak; remove first hand/foot and dry, and soak the second hand/foot. 2. **Cuticle care** involves applying cuticle remover cream, pushing back cuticles, trimming cuticles/hangnails if necessary, cleaning under the free edge and brushing the nails. 3. **Exfoliate** client's feet to remove dead skin cells (pedicure). 4. **Massage** lower arm and hand or lower leg and foot (repeat on both sides). 5. **Polish** nails beginning with base coat, then colored polish (if desired) and top coat.
NATURAL NAIL SERVICE COMPLETION	» Reinforce client's satisfaction with overall salon experience. » Make professional product recommendations. » Prebook client's next appointment. » End client's visit with warm and personal goodbye. » Discard single-use supplies; disinfect tools and multi-use supplies; disinfect workstation and arrange in proper order. » Complete client record. » Wash hands.

NATURAL NAIL RUBRICS

A performance rubric is a document that identifies defined criteria at which levels of performance can be measured objectively. Each natural nail rubric is an example that your instructor might choose to use for scoring. Each natural nail service rubric is divided into three main areas—Preparation, Procedure and Completion. Each area is further divided into step-by-step procedures that will ensure client safety and satisfaction.

BASIC MANICURE RUBRIC

Allotted Time: 30 Minutes

Student Name:_____ ID Number: _____

Instructor: _____ Date: _____ Start Time: _____ End Time: _____

BASIC MANICURE   (Live Model) – Each scoring item is marked with either a "Yes" or a "No." Each "Yes" counts for one point. Total number of points attainable is 33.

CRITERIA	YES	NO	INSTRUCTOR ASSESSMENT
PREPARATION: Did student...			
1. Set up workstation with properly labeled supplies?	☐	☐	
2. Place disinfected tools and supplies at a visibly clean workstation?	☐	☐	
3. Wash their hands?	☐	☐	
Connect: Did student...			
4. Meet and greet client with a welcoming smile and pleasant tone of voice?	☐	☐	
5. Communicate to build rapport and develop a relationship with client?	☐	☐	
6. Refer to client by name throughout service?	☐	☐	
Consult: Did student...			
7. Ask questions to discover client's wants and needs?	☐	☐	
8. Gain feedback and consent from client before proceeding?	☐	☐	
PROCEDURE: Did student...			
9. Ask client to wash hands and perform thorough visual analysis of skin and nails?	☐	☐	
10. Remove polish and analyze client's hands and nails and check for any contraindications?	☐	☐	
Create: Did student...			
11. File and shape nails to the agreed-upon length and shape?	☐	☐	
12. Place hand in fingerbowl to soak and repeat filing and shaping on the second hand?	☐	☐	
13. Remove first hand and dry, then place second hand in fingerbowl?	☐	☐	
14. Apply cuticle cream, push back cuticles and nip, if necessary?	☐	☐	
15. Clean under free edge?	☐	☐	
16. Remove second hand and dry brush nails on the first hand, and, then repeat cuticle care on the second hand?	☐	☐	
17. Apply massage lotion to client's entire hand, wrist and lower arm?	☐	☐	
18. Perform hand and arm massage and repeat massage on the second hand?	☐	☐	
19. Remove lotion from nail plates?	☐	☐	
20. Apply base coat?	☐	☐	
21. Apply colored polish?	☐	☐	
22. Apply top coat?	☐	☐	
23. Apply speed dry and cuticle oil?	☐	☐	
24. Practice infection control procedures and safety guidelines throughout service?	☐	☐	
COMPLETION (Complete): Did student...			
25. Ask questions and look for verbal and nonverbal cues to determine client's level of satisfaction?	☐	☐	
26. Make professional product recommendations?	☐	☐	
27. Ask client to make a future appointment?	☐	☐	
28. End client's visit with a warm and personal goodbye?	☐	☐	
29. Discard single-use supplies?	☐	☐	
30. Disinfect tools and multi-use supplies; disinfect workstation and arrange in proper order?	☐	☐	
31. Complete service within scheduled time?	☐	☐	
32. Complete client record?	☐	☐	
33. Wash their hands following the service?	☐	☐	

COMMENTS: _____   TOTAL POINTS = _____ ÷ 33 = _____ %

BASIC PEDICURE RUBRIC

Allotted Time: 45 Minutes

Student Name: _____ ID Number: _____

Instructor: _____ Date: _____ Start Time: _____ End Time: _____

BASIC PEDICURE (Live Model) — Each scoring item is marked with either a "Yes" or a "No." Each "Yes" counts for one point. Total number of points attainable is 35.

CRITERIA	YES	NO	INSTRUCTOR ASSESSMENT
PREPARATION: Did student...			
1. Set up workstation with properly labeled supplies?	☐	☐	
2. Place disinfected tools and supplies at a visibly clean workstation?	☐	☐	
3. Wash their hands?	☐	☐	
Connect: Did student...			
4. Meet and greet client with a welcoming smile and pleasant tone of voice?	☐	☐	
5. Communicate to build rapport and develop a relationship with client?	☐	☐	
6. Refer to client by name throughout service?	☐	☐	
Consult: Did student...			
7. Ask questions to discover client's wants and needs?	☐	☐	
8. Gain feedback and consent from client before proceeding?	☐	☐	
PROCEDURE: Did student...			
9. Sanitize and analyze client's feet and check for any contraindications?	☐	☐	
Create: Did student...			
10. Place client's feet in footbath and allow to soak for 5-10 minutes?	☐	☐	
11. Remove both feet and dry?	☐	☐	
12. Remove nail polish and analyze toenails?	☐	☐	
13. Trim and file nails on the first foot, return to foot bath, then repeat on opposite foot?	☐	☐	
14. Remove foot from footbath, apply cuticle cream on first foot and push back cuticles?	☐	☐	
15. Clean under free edge and brush nails?	☐	☐	
16. Remove second foot from footbath, dry and repeat cuticle care?	☐	☐	
17. Apply foot scrub or sloughing lotion and massage, then place foot back in footbath and repeat on opposite foot?	☐	☐	
18. Remove both feet from footbath and dry?	☐	☐	
19. Massage foot and leg with lotion and repeat on the opposite side?	☐	☐	
20. Remove lotion from nail plates of both feet?	☐	☐	
21. Place pedicure slippers on feet and position toe separators?	☐	☐	
22. Apply base coat to nails of both feet?	☐	☐	
23. Apply colored polish to nails of both feet?	☐	☐	
24. Apply top coat to nails of both feet?	☐	☐	
25. Apply speed dry and cuticle oil?	☐	☐	
26. Practice infection control procedures and safety guidelines throughout service?	☐	☐	
COMPLETION (Complete): Did student...			
27. Ask questions and look for verbal and nonverbal cues to determine client's level of satisfaction?	☐	☐	
28. Make professional product recommendations?	☐	☐	
29. Ask client to make a future appointment?	☐	☐	
30. End client's visit with a warm and personal goodbye?	☐	☐	
31. Discard single-use supplies?	☐	☐	
32. Disinfect tools and multi-use supplies; disinfect workstation and arrange in proper order?	☐	☐	
33. Complete service within scheduled time?	☐	☐	
34. Complete client record?	☐	☐	
35. Wash their hands following the service?	☐	☐	

COMMENTS: _____ TOTAL POINTS = _____ ÷ 35 = _____ %

SALON**CONNECTION**

It's the Little Things...

It's important to always pay attention to details. Timing is important, but don't skip the little things. This could turn your client's visit into a mediocre experience rather than the excellent service they come to expect from you as a salon professional.

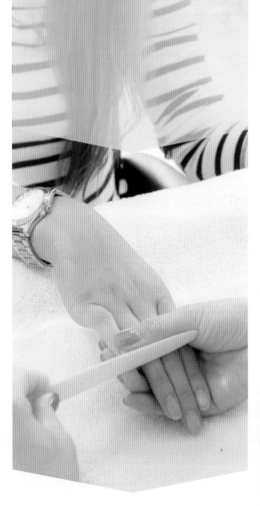

DISCOVER**MORE**

Personal Touch

Do some research online or by talking to other salon professionals. What do they do to make their natural nail services stand out from others? Do they provide aromatherapy or maybe warm towels during a pedicure? Do they offer a hot stone massage, or do they have a signature massage technique? Find a few ideas to try out on your next manicure or pedicure client.

LESSONS LEARNED

» Procedural guidelines to follow when performing a natural nail service include:

  » File and shape nails from the corner to the center, making sure they are all the same length and shape.

  » Push back cuticles using light, quick circular movements.

  » Exfoliate (pedicure) the feet to remove dead skin cells and soften skin.

  » Maintain contact during a massage using an even tempo and pressure and making sure to gently remove hands at the end.

  » Apply polish holding the finger or toe tightly and pinching to move the sidewalls away from the nail plate.

» The three areas of a natural nail service include the Preparation, Procedure and Completion:

  » Preparation includes setting up the workstation with disinfected tools and implements and connecting with the client.

  » Procedure includes ensuring client safety and performing the natural nail service.

  » Completion includes reinforcing client's satisfaction, recommending products, asking client to make a future appointment, disinfecting workstation and completing the client record.

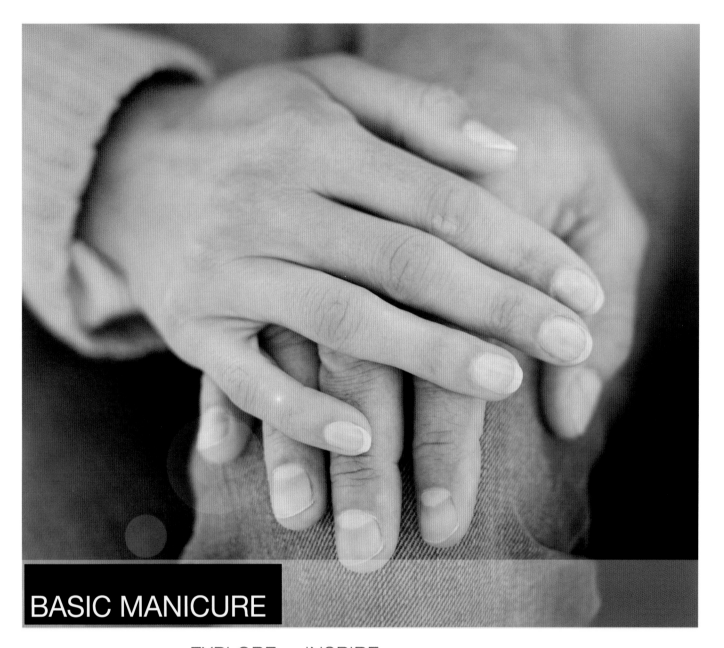

BASIC MANICURE

EXPLORE

Why do you think a manicure is a good way to introduce clients to additional services?

INSPIRE

A basic manicure is the foundation for all other nail care services.

ACHIEVE

Following this *Basic Manicure Workshop*, you'll be able to:

» Perform a basic manicure

PERFORMANCE GUIDE

BASIC MANICURE

View the video, then perform this workshop. Complete the self-check as you progress through the workshop.

30 mins
Suggested
Salon Speed

PREPARATION	✓

» Assemble tools and products
» Set up workstation
» Wash your hands
» Ask client to wash hands

☐

1. Remove polish and perform a visual analysis of the hands and nails:

» Consult with client about desired shape and length of nails

Note: To efficiently remove polish, wipe from base of nail to tip to avoid leaving polish residue on skin.

☐

FILE	

2. File and shape the nails on first hand:

» Determine nail shape
» Trim nails if necessary
» File corner to center

☐

3. Place hand in finger bowl.

☐

4. Repeat file and shape on second hand (Step 2).

☐

5. Remove first hand and dry. ☐

6. Place second hand in finger bowl. ☐

CUTICLE CARE

7. Apply cuticle cream. ☐

8. **Push back cuticles:**
» Use light, quick, circular movements along cuticle
» Nip cuticles/hangnails if necessary

   Note: Follow your area's regulatory guidelines
   for trimming cuticles. ☐

9. **Clean under free edge.** ☐

10. **Remove second hand from finger bowl and brush nails of first hand:**
» Hold hand over finger bowl to remove any remaining bits of cuticle
» Dry both hands ☐

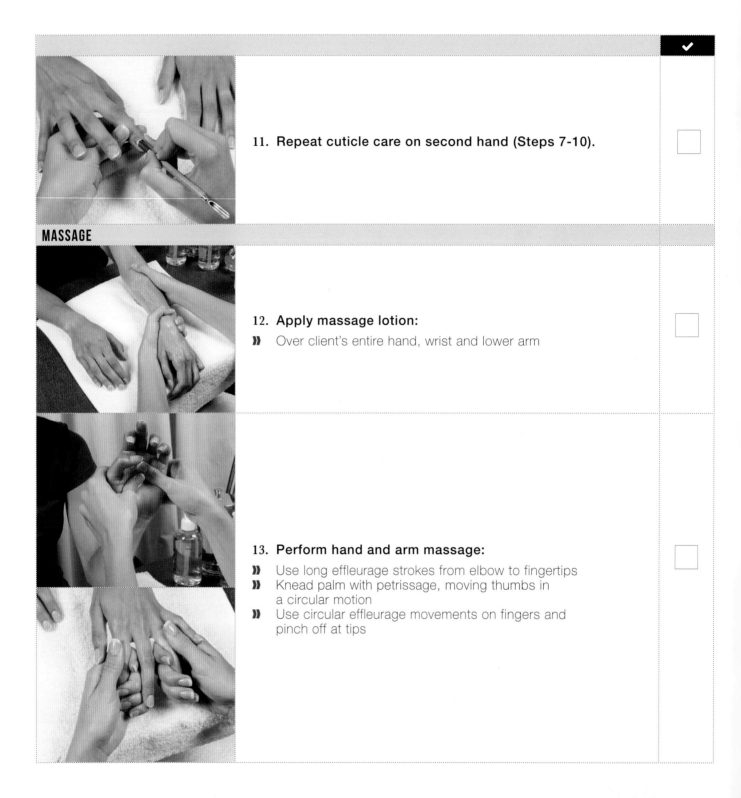

11. **Repeat cuticle care on second hand (Steps 7-10).**

MASSAGE

12. **Apply massage lotion:**
» Over client's entire hand, wrist and lower arm

13. **Perform hand and arm massage:**
» Use long effleurage strokes from elbow to fingertips
» Knead palm with petrissage, moving thumbs in a circular motion
» Use circular effleurage movements on fingers and pinch off at tips

14. **Repeat massage on second hand (Steps 12 and 13).**

15. **Remove lotion from nail plates:**
    » Use lint-free wipe or cotton
    » Saturate with nail preparation solution or polish remover

16. **Apply base coat:**
    » Apply to nails of both hands

17. **Apply colored polish, if applicable:**
    » First coat of color to nails of both hands
    » Second coat of color to nails of both hands
    » Apply polish to free edge

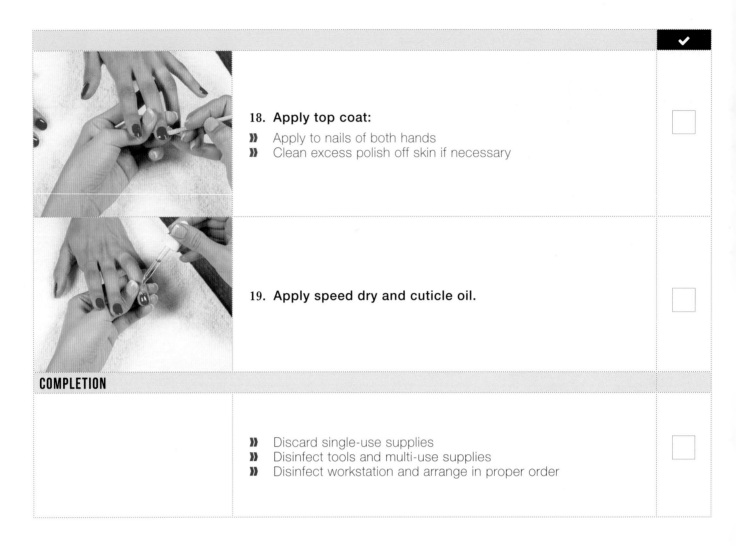

✔

18. **Apply top coat:**
» Apply to nails of both hands
» Clean excess polish off skin if necessary

☐

19. **Apply speed dry and cuticle oil.**

☐

COMPLETION

» Discard single-use supplies
» Disinfect tools and multi-use supplies
» Disinfect workstation and arrange in proper order

☐

30 mins
Suggested Salon Speed

My Speed

INSTRUCTIONS:
Record your time in comparison with the suggested salon speed. Then, list here how you could improve your performance.

_____
_____
_____
_____
_____

BASIC PEDICURE

EXPLORE

Have you ever received a relaxing pedicure? How can you provide that same type of service to your clients?

INSPIRE

Attention to the health and care of the feet and nails during a basic pedicure can be valuable to your clients' overall health and well-being.

ACHIEVE

Following this *Basic Pedicure Workshop*, you'll be able to:

» Perform a basic pedicure

PERFORMANCE GUIDE

BASIC PEDICURE

View the video, then perform this workshop. Complete the self-check as you progress through the workshop.

45 mins
Suggested
Salon Speed

PREPARATION	✔

» Assemble tools and products
» Set up workstation
» Wash your hands

☐

1. Sanitize client's feet:
» Use a waterless sanitizer or antiseptic spray
» Wear gloves if required by your area's regulating agency

☐

2. Perform a visual analysis of feet:
» Perform visual analysis of nails if not polished

☐

3. Place client's feet in footbath:
» Soak 5-10 minutes

☐

4. Remove both feet and dry. ☐

5. Remove nail polish and perform a visual analysis of nails. ☐

FILE

6. **File and shape nails on first foot:** ☐

   » Trim nails if necessary, straight across
   » File straight across, softening corners

7. **Place foot in footbath.** ☐

8. Repeat file and shape (Steps 6-7). ☐

9. Remove first foot and dry. ☐

10. Place second foot in footbath. ☐

CUTICLE CARE

11. Apply cuticle cream. ☐

12. **Push back cuticles:** ☐
» Use light, quick, circular movements along cuticle
» Nip cuticles/hangnails if necessary

    Note: Follow your area's regulatory guidelines
    for trimming cuticles.

13. Clean under free edge and brush nails on first foot. Place foot in footbath.

14. Remove second foot, dry, repeat cuticle care (Steps 11-13).

EXFOLIATE

15. Remove first foot from footbath and dry. Apply foot scrub or sloughing lotion:
    » Apply product over client's entire foot
    » Massage to remove dead skin cells

16. Use a foot file if needed and place foot back in footbath.

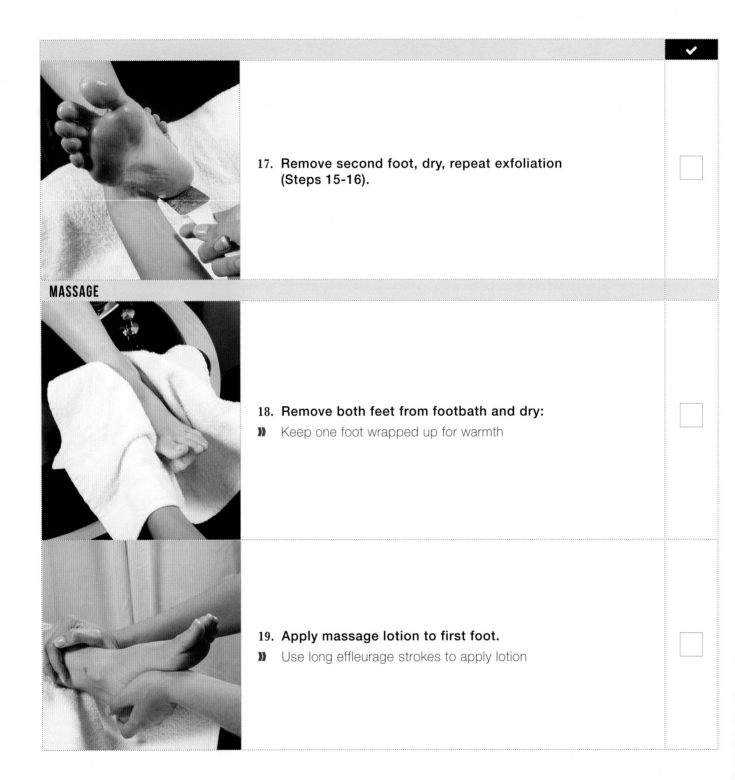

17. **Remove second foot, dry, repeat exfoliation (Steps 15-16).**

MASSAGE

18. **Remove both feet from footbath and dry:**
» Keep one foot wrapped up for warmth

19. **Apply massage lotion to first foot.**
» Use long effleurage strokes to apply lotion

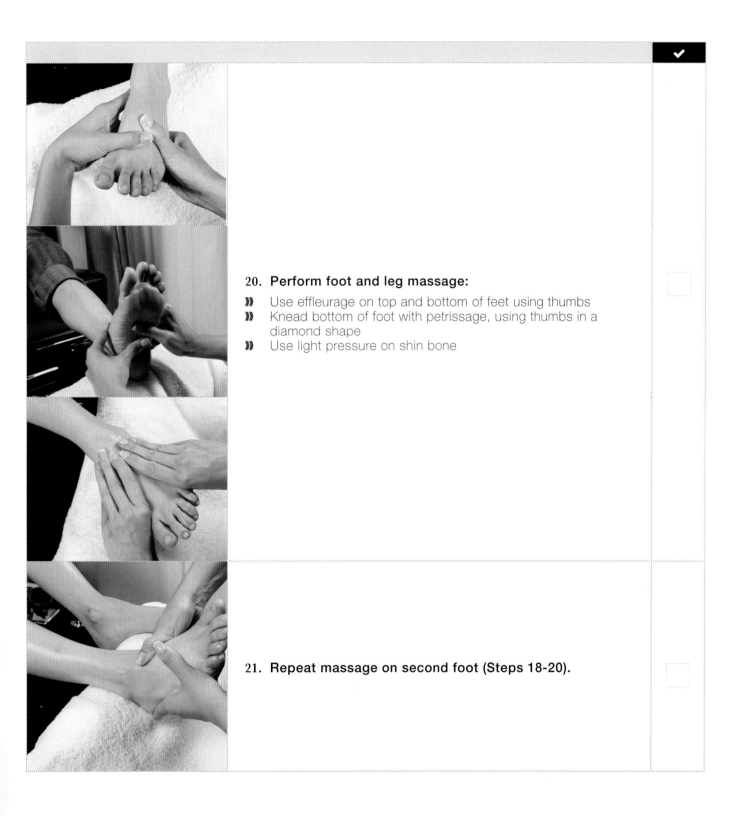

20. **Perform foot and leg massage:**
   » Use effleurage on top and bottom of feet using thumbs
   » Knead bottom of foot with petrissage, using thumbs in a diamond shape
   » Use light pressure on shin bone

21. **Repeat massage on second foot (Steps 18-20).**

POLISH ✓

22. Remove lotion from nail plates:
» Use lint-free wipe or cotton
» Saturate with nail preparation solution or polish remover

23. Place pedicure slippers on client's feet, then position toe separators.

24. Apply base coat:
» Apply to nails of both feet

25. Apply colored polish (if applicable):
» First coat of color to nails of both feet
» Second coat of color to nails of both feet
» Apply polish to free edge

26. Apply top coat:
» Apply to nails of both feet
» Clean excess polish off skin if necessary

27. Apply speed dry and cuticle oil.

» Discard single-use supplies
» Disinfect tools and multi-use supplies
» Disinfect workstation and arrange in proper order

45 mins
Suggested
Salon Speed

My Speed
_____
_____
_____

INSTRUCTIONS:
Record your time in comparison with the suggested salon speed. Then, list here how you could improve your performance.

_____
_____
_____
_____
_____

113^c.8

ARTIFICIAL
NAIL SYSTEM

PRODUCTS AND
ESSENTIALS

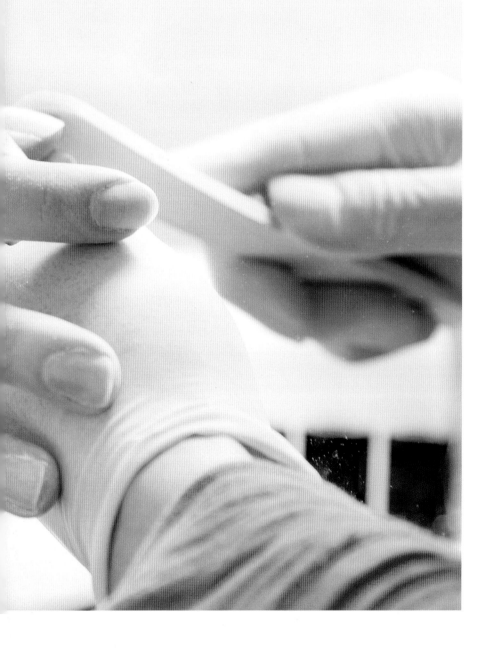

EXPLORE //

What are some ways artificial nails are formed?

INSPIRE //

Knowing how artificial nail products work and their different application and maintenance options helps you offer the best services for your clients.

ACHIEVE //

Following this lesson on *Artificial Nail System Products and Essentials*, you'll be able to:

» Identify the two types of artificial nail systems

» Describe artificial nail preparation and why it is important

» Identify the different artificial nail basics and describe them in your own words

» Describe the different artificial removal methods in your own words

FOCUS //

ARTIFICIAL NAIL SYSTEM PRODUCTS AND ESSENTIALS

Artificial Nail Systems

Artificial Nail Preparation

Artificial Nail Basics

Artificial Nail Removal

113ᶜ.8 | ARTIFICIAL NAIL SYSTEM PRODUCTS AND ESSENTIALS

ARTIFICIAL NAIL SYSTEMS

Artificial nail systems refer to the essential products, tools and supplies that are needed to create artificial nails. Sometimes called nail enhancements, artificial nails are used to change or improve the appearance of the nails and help to conceal broken nails. There are several types of artificial nail products currently available for use in the salon. Each has special procedures individualized by the manufacturer of the product. Since these popular services require regular maintenance, they can help you build your clientele and profitability in the salon.

There are two main types of artificial nail systems used today:

1. Acrylic nails (powder and liquid)

2. Gel nails (light-cured)

ACRYLIC NAILS

Acrylic nail enhancements have been a staple in the nail industry for decades. An acrylic nail is created by using a combination of an acrylic powder called polymer and an acrylic liquid called monomer. A sable brush is first dipped into the liquid and then the powder to create a bead, or ball, of acrylic on the end or side of the brush. The bead is then pressed into place on the nail to create the overlay or sculptured nail.

All artificial nail products contain monomers and polymers, and most often you will hear these terms referred to in acrylic liquid-and-powder systems. However, keep in mind that all artificial nail enhancement products contain some type of monomers and polymers.

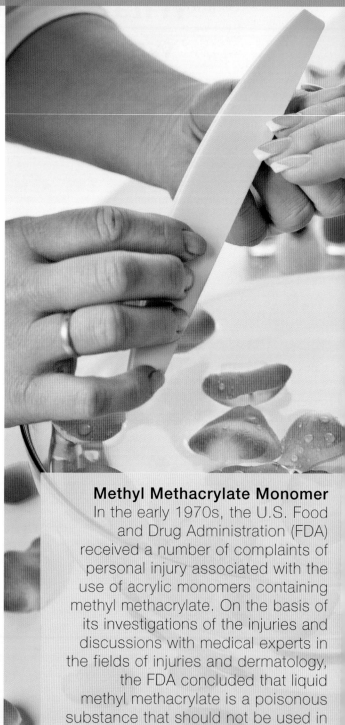

Methyl Methacrylate Monomer
In the early 1970s, the U.S. Food and Drug Administration (FDA) received a number of complaints of personal injury associated with the use of acrylic monomers containing methyl methacrylate. On the basis of its investigations of the injuries and discussions with medical experts in the fields of injuries and dermatology, the FDA concluded that liquid methyl methacrylate is a poisonous substance that should not be used in acrylic monomers. However, methyl methacrylate is safe to use in acrylic polymers.

Liquid Monomer

Most liquid monomers, also known as acrylic liquids, have several types of monomers which offer different properties. Typically, ethyl methacrylate is used as the primary monomer in acrylic liquid. Others include:

» Acrylic monomers

» Cross-linking monomers
  » Added to create a strong network

  » Dimethacrylate and trimethacrylate are commonly used

Other additives that may be contained within the liquid monomer are:

» Catalysts
  » Speed up the chemical reaction

» Inhibitors
  » used as preservatives that keep the monomers from "setting up" or curing on their own

  » Properly inhibited liquids will last one to two years before the inhibitor runs out; this will also happen if it becomes contaminated or is exposed to heat or sunlight

» Dyes

» Plasticizers

» UV-protective color stabilizers

Acrylic monomer does not begin polymerization, or the curing of the product, until it is mixed with the powder polymer..

Powder Polymer

Most powder polymers, or acrylic powders, contain:

» Polymers

» Initiators
  » Necessary for the liquid monomer to begin its chemical reaction

Others also contain:

» Pigments
  » To give color

» Silica
  » To keep powder free-flowing

ACRYLIC PRODUCTS AND ESSENTIALS

ACRYLIC PRODUCTS		DESCRIPTION	FUNCTION
	MONOMER	Liquid in form	Mixes with the powder to form an acrylic nail
	POLYMER	Powder in form, comes in many colors	Mixes with the monomer to form an acrylic nail
	ACRYLIC PRIMER	Liquid in form; either contains methacrylic acid or is considered acid free	Ensures adhesion of acrylic product to nail; dehydrating product

Make sure nails are completely dry before applying artificial nails. This avoids trapped moisture and bacterial infection. Most primers contain ingredients to prevent bacteria growth, so avoid touching the nails after primer has been applied.

ACRYLIC PRODUCTS AND ESSENTIALS

TOOLS/IMPLEMENTS		DESCRIPTION	FUNCTION
	DAPPEN DISH	Small glass container	Holds monomer and polymer separately
	ACRYLIC BRUSH	Made from natural hair, typically sable; can be flat, oval or rounded; many sizes available	Used to hold the monomer and polymer to build the acrylic nail; used to manipulate the product to the desired location

SUPPLIES		DESCRIPTION	FUNCTION
	NAIL FILE	An abrasive in a variety of different grits, or number of abrasive granules per square inch	Shortens, files and shapes artificial nails
		» File Grit	» Purpose
		» Coarse (80-120)	» Removes length on enhancements; removes excess product for artificial nail maintenance
		» Medium (130-240)	» Shapes any nail and refines surface of enhancements
		» Fine (250-900)	» Shapes and refines surface of any nail
		» Extra-Fine	» Smooths surface imperfections on any nail; shines nails
	BUFFER	Extra-fine file	Smooths nails; shines surface of nail
	EYEDROPPER	Glass or plastic dropper	Used to move acrylic liquid from container to dappen dish
	DISPOSABLE TOWEL	Lint-free single-use towel	Used to protect the table and used for cleaning and removing excess product from brushes

LIGHT-CURED GEL NAILS

When observing the finished look of gel nails next to acrylic nails, it would be difficult to determine which product was initially applied. The two look and feel very similar once finished. However, one major distinction between gel nails and acrylic nails is the way they harden, or cure. With acrylics, the chemical reaction between the powder and liquid acrylics causes the product to dry and harden on its own. Gel products, on the other hand, do not fully harden or cure until they are exposed to either an ultraviolet (UV), LED or halogen light.

Another difference is that gel products are in a gel-like form rather than a powder-and-liquid mixture. Since gel does not cure until it is exposed to light, it's important to keep the nails level to keep the product from moving. To make it easier for the client to keep the nails level, gel is first applied to the pinky finger through the index finger and cured. The thumbs are done separately and placed under the light together. Similar to acrylics, gels are available in many different colors and can be used as an overlay for natural nails or tips and can also be used to sculpt a nail.

Gel systems are different from acrylics in two ways:

1. Product comes in gel form, which doesn't require the combining of a liquid and a powder

2. Product requires exposure to a light source to cure (harden)

Gels are mainly made of acrylic oligomers. An oligomer is a short chain version of a polymer. While a polymer may have thousands or millions of monomer links, an oligomer consists of a limited number of monomer links—anywhere from five to 500.

POLYMER:	POLY = MANY	= **SOLID**
MONOMER:	MONO = ONE	= **LIQUID**
OLIGOMER:	OLIGO = FEW	= **GEL**

All light-cured gels use photo initiators to begin the curing process. Gels can also contain a wide variety of other ingredients depending on their use:

» Base gels, also referred to as gel primers, contain priming molecules.

» Some gels may have monomers for thinning and speeding up the curing process.

   » For example, for a smooth finish, a sealer, also called a finishing gel, is applied on top of the gel nail causing it to self-level, or spread evenly on its own.

   » A building, or sculpting, gel used to create the artificial nails may contain silica or polymers for thickening so they will hold their shape.

   » Some gels may contain cross-linking monomers; however, most oligomers used in gels are diacrylates or dimethacrylates, which act as their own cross-linkers.

   » Some also contain pigments to give color.

GEL PRODUCTS AND ESSENTIALS

GEL PRODUCTS		DESCRIPTION	FUNCTION
	GEL	Gel in form, comes in many colors and different viscosities (thicknesses)	Acrylic-based product used to form a gel nail, high viscosity (thick) gel used for sculpting, lower viscosity (thinner) gel used for overlays
	GEL BONDER OR PRIMER	Thin gel or liquid in form	Ensures adhesion of gel product to nail
	GEL SEALER	Thin gel product	Creates a high-shine finish and seals product

GEL PRODUCTS AND ESSENTIALS

TOOLS/IMPLEMENTS		DESCRIPTION	FUNCTION
	GEL BRUSH	Made from synthetic fibers; can be many different shapes and sizes	Used to apply product to the nail and manipulate the product to the desired location

SUPPLIES		DESCRIPTION	FUNCTION
	NAIL FILE	An abrasive in a variety of different grits, or number of abrasive granules per square inch	Shortens, files and shapes artificial nails
		» File Grit	» Purpose
		» Coarse (80-120)	» Removes length on enhancements; removes excess product for artificial nail maintenance
		» Medium (130-240)	» Shapes any nail and refines surface of enhancements
		» Fine (250-900)	» Shapes and refines surface of any nail
		» Extra-Fine	» Smooths surface imperfections on any nail; shines nails
	BUFFER	Extra-fine file	Smooths nails; shines surface of nail
	DISPOSABLE TOWEL	Lint-free single-use towel	Used to protect the table and used for cleaning and removing excess product from brushes

Adhesives:

Adhesives are glue-like products that create a bond between two incompatible surfaces, such as a nail tip and the nail plate. For an adhesive to work effectively, it must be compatible with the two surfaces it bonds together. For example, ordinary school glue is made to bond porous surfaces like paper, cloth and wood. But if this same adhesive is used to bond two pieces of plastic, the bond can be broken with little force because it is not porous. However, when used on paper the bond is very strong and the paper will tear before the bond is broken. Nail adhesives are created to be compatible with the keratin in the nail and common materials found in nail enhancement products.

Nail wraps are a service that has become less popular over the years, but clients might still have questions about it. Nail wraps involve using an overlay of a type of fabric (silk, fiberglass, linen or nylon) secured with a thick adhesive, referred to as resin, and an accelerator to speed the curing process. The small piece of the fabric is adhered to the nail with the resin, and then reinforced with two to three additional layers of resin. Nail wraps can be worn over natural nails or over tips for added length. They have also been used to repair longer nails that crack or break.

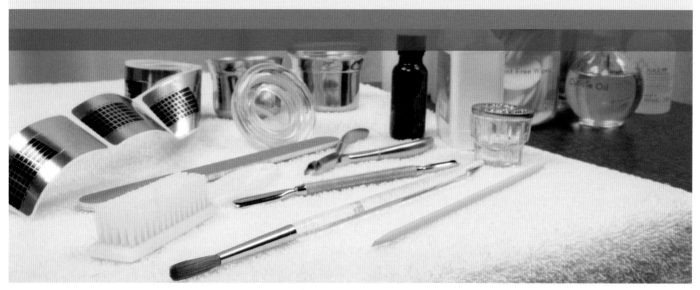

ARTIFICIAL NAIL PREPARATION

Prior to any artificial nail service, a basic dry manicure, or "waterless" manicure, should be performed. A dry manicure is a basic manicure procedure performed without soaking the nails or the massage steps. The process is then followed by the removal of "shine" (oil and residue) from the surface of the nail plate. It is important not to touch the nail once the nail plate has been prepared in order to avoid transferring oil back onto the nail plate.

» If there is moisture on the nail plate before applying artificial nails, many problems may occur, such as lifting (when the product does not adhere to the nail plate) or a bacterial infection due to trapped moisture.

	CUTICLE CARE	**Perform basic manicure without soaking nails and massaging hands:** » Apply cuticle remover cream to area using either a cotton-tipped orangewood stick, cotton swab or dropper » Use light, quick circular movements in cuticle area » Spray nails with water or recommended product and wipe each nail plate with towel to remove all traces of cuticle cream
	**FILE**	**File the free edge:** » Create a rounded nail shape prior to tip application for best fit (if applicable) » Remove shine from nail plate using 240-grit or higher file » Clean debris and dust from nail plate using manufacturer's recommended nail preparation solution

ARTIFICIAL NAIL BASICS

Salon clients request artificial nails for a number of reasons. Many use nail enhancements to strengthen and lengthen weak nails. They are also used for concealing or repairing chipped or broken nails. In this section you will learn about the different application methods of artificial nails as well as maintenance and removal. Along with the application of artificial nails the regular maintenance will serve as an excellent way to build your clientele and increase your profitability.

Artificial nails can be applied over tips and directly on the nail, or built on top of a nail form. Nail forms are temporary attachments that are placed under the free edge of the natural nail to help create and sculpt an artificial nail and free edge. These two types of application are known as: overlay and sculptured nails.

Common terms to refer to areas of the nail when applying artificial nails are:

Zone 1: Free edge
Zone 2: Apex or stress area of the nail
Zone 3: Cuticle area

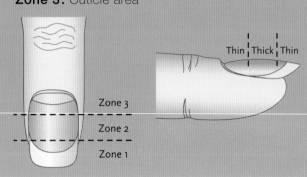

OVERLAY – CREATED BY APPLYING ANY ARTIFICIAL PRODUCT OVER THE NATURAL NAIL OR A NAIL TIP

SCULPTURED – ACRYLIC OR GEL PRODUCT BUILT ON TOP OF A NAIL FORM

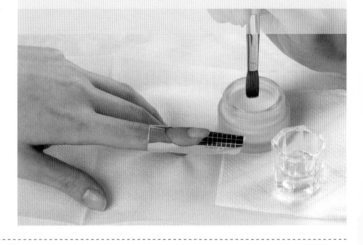

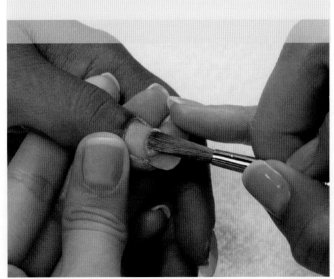

OVERLAY

An overlay is the application of acrylic or gel on the natural nail or over nail tips if added length is desired. Overlays can give the client a very natural looking nail enhancement. An overlay can be performed with a single-color or two-color application. The typical two-color application uses pink and white to create a French manicure look.

Nail Tips

The length of your client's natural nail can be extended using nail tips. Nail tips are plastic, nylon or acetate fingernail-shaped extensions that are applied to the natural nail using a nail adhesive. Nail tips can provide a temporary length enhancement, but they are more often used as a base for acrylic or gel products. Nail tips without an overlay are considered temporary because the stress area is weak without an overlay to strengthen it.

There are many different varieties of nail tips available today. They come in many shapes, sizes and colors.

Nail tips have two important structural features:

1. Tip well: The area that adheres to the natural nail plate

2. Position stop: A ridge underneath the nail tip where the free edge of the natural nail fits into place

There are two types of tip wells: full-wells and half-wells. The tip well should cover no more than half the nail plate since the length of the natural nail determines which type to use. For example, a long natural nail bed may require the use of a full-well tip, while a short natural nail bed may only need a half-well tip. To achieve the best fit, it is recommended to give the natural nails a more rounded shape prior to nail tip application. A round-shaped nail tends to fit better against the position stop.

These come in sizes often numbered from 1-10, with number 1 being the largest and 10 the smallest. Selecting the right size for each of your client's nails is an important step in ensuring that they fit well and adhere properly.

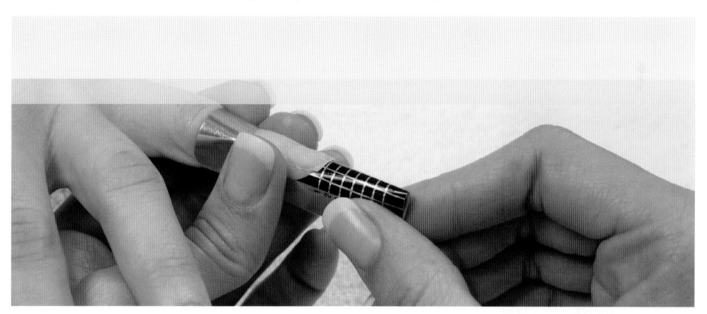

SCULPTURED NAILS

Sculptured nails are created over a nail form rather than using a tip for added length. The nail form fits snugly under the free edge of the natural nail and then acrylic or gel is used to create a nail. After the product hardens, or cures the nail form is removed. Sculptured nails can also be created with a single-color or two-color method.

ARTIFICIAL NAIL MAINTENANCE

All artificial nail services require maintenance to keep them looking nice, as well as keep them healthy for the client. If artificial nails are not maintained on a regular basis they can lift and create the perfect breeding ground for bacteria. Artificial nails need a fill every 10-14 days depending on how quickly your client's nails grow, as well as how often the enhancements are exposed to water or other harsh conditions. As the natural nails grow, the enhancement grows out with the natural nail, leaving the area at the cuticle without product and the nail structure unbalanced.

Two-Week Maintenance

As the natural nail is exposed at the cuticle area (Zone 3), it is necessary to re-balance the nail.

This is done by applying acrylic or gel to the cuticle area and making sure the nails are repaired if there are any cracks or broken nails.

	PREPARE NAILS	**Perform basic manicure without soaking nails and massaging hands:** » Check for cracks or any lifting or separation of product » If cracks, lifting or separation are present, carefully file away product from the area
	FILE	**Blend "old product" with new growth using 180-grit file or higher to eliminate line of demarcation:** » Concentrate on product: Only remove shine on natural nail using 240-grit file » Hold file flat against nail to prevent damaging natural nail » Prepare the nail with proper products according to manufacturer's instructions
	APPLY	**Apply product evenly and smoothly to new growth area or Zone 3:** » Blend product with previously applied product » Avoid touching cuticle with product
	BALANCE AND FINISH	**File using long strokes and light pressure:** » File to keep Zones 1 and 3 thinnest and Zone 2 thickest » Check for client's comfort while filing » Remove all debris from filing before polishing or buffing to a shine

Four-Week Maintenance

Four-week maintenance applies to two-color acrylic or gel nails. As previously mentioned, the artificial nail moves forward with the nail growth in the cuticle area. This makes the smile line move forward on the nail so it no longer covers the natural smile line near the tip of the nail.

The four-week maintenance differs from the two-week maintenance because not only is the new growth area filled in, but the smile line is also repositioned.

	PREPARE NAILS	**Perform basic manicure without soaking nails and massaging hands:** » Check for cracks or any lifting or separation of product » If cracks, lifting or separation are present, carefully file away product from the area
	FILE	**Blend "old product" with new growth using 180-grit file or higher to eliminate line of demarcation and thin the free edge to replace product at free edge:** » Concentrate on product: Only remove shine on natural nail using 240-grit file » Hold file flat against nail to prevent damaging natural nail » Prepare the nail with proper products according to manufacturer's instructions
	APPLY	**Apply product to Zone 1:** » Create a new smile line **Apply product to Zone 2:** » Blend Zone 2 with Zone 1 **Apply product to Zone 3:** » Blend Zone 3 with Zone 2
	BALANCE AND FINISH	**File using long strokes and light pressure:** » File to keep Zones 1 and 3 thinnest and Zone 2 thickest » Check for client's comfort while filing » Remove all debris from filing before polishing or buffing to a shine

ARTIFICIAL NAIL REMOVAL

Knowing how to correctly and safely remove artificial nails will help preserve the health of your clients' natural nails. Make sure your clients know to have their enhancements removed professionally rather than trying to remove them on their own.

ACRYLIC NAIL REMOVAL

There are several types of artificial nail product removers. The most widely used solvent in the nail industry is acetone. Acetone is a clear, highly flammable liquid solvent, which is used in both nail polish removers and artificial nail product removers. Although acetone is an effective solvent, it can dissolve the skin's natural oils and dry out the skin. However, there are specific product removers on the market that contain other ingredients along with the acetone to counteract the drying effects.

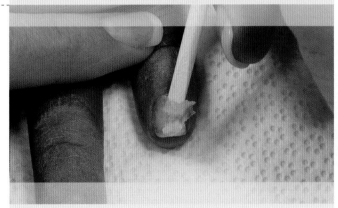

GEL NAIL REMOVAL

Unlike acrylics, the chemical makeup of tradition gel nails, makes it impossible for them to be dissolved by acetone or any other solvent. Instead, gel nails are properly removed by gently filing the product away. Extra caution is necessary when filing to preserve the health of the natural nail and to not over-file and thin the nail plate.

>> Be guided by your area's regulatory agency for proper disposal of used chemicals. **DO NOT** pour them down the sink or toilet, on the ground, down outside drains, or onto cotton balls. Some chemicals have specific disposal requirements. For example, used liquid acetone must be saved in a fire department-approved metal container and disposed of as hazardous waste.

SALON**CONNECTION**
Let the Nails
Fit the Client

When a client comes in requesting artificial nails it is your decision as a professional to suggest the type of artificial nail that would be best for them. Sometimes it is a personal preference either by the client or the salon professional. Other times it may depend on the overall condition of the client's nails or past experience with either acrylic or gel nails. If one product is not working the way you would like on the client's nails you can try the other. Or if a client has a sensitivity to acrylic, you would want to use gel for their enhancements.

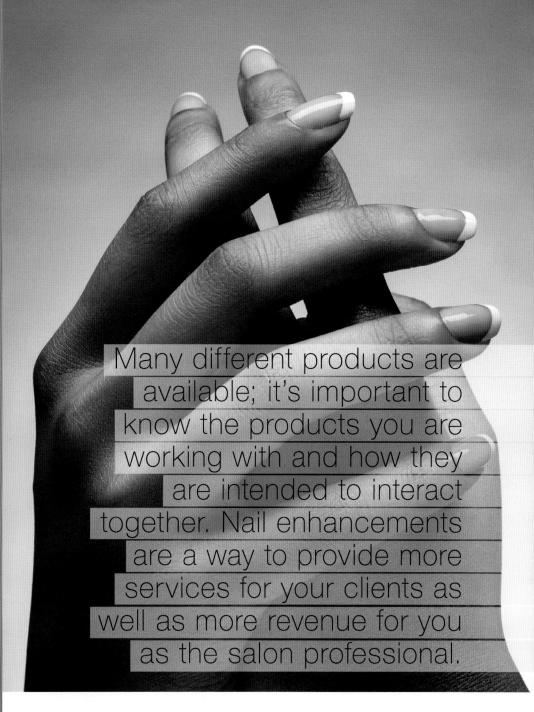

Many different products are available; it's important to know the products you are working with and how they are intended to interact together. Nail enhancements are a way to provide more services for your clients as well as more revenue for you as the salon professional.

LESSONS LEARNED

» Two main types of artificial nail systems are acrylic nail systems and light-cured gel nail systems.

» Artificial nail preparation includes the basic cuticle care and filing steps of a manicure and are performed to ensure that all oils and residue are removed from the nail plate prior to application.

» Artificial nail basics include an overlay application on natural nails or nail tips, sculptured nails and the two-week and four week maintenance for both.

» Removal of acrylic nails is performed by soaking nails in an acetone-based remover and carefully pushing product from the nail as it dissolves while gel nail removal involves carefully filing the old product from the nails.

EXPLORE //

What step in the artificial nail process do you think contributes most to a beautiful and satisfying finish?

ARTIFICIAL
NAIL
SERVICE
113ᶜ.9

INSPIRE //

Artificial nail service procedures provide you with a structure and guidelines that will help you stay organized and attentive to your client's comfort.

ACHIEVE //

Following this lesson on *Artificial Nail Service*, you'll be able to:

» Provide examples of guidelines to follow when performing an artificial nail service

» Describe the three areas of an artificial nail service

FOCUS //

ARTIFICIAL NAIL SERVICE

Artificial Nail Client Guidelines

Artificial Nail Service Overview

Artificial Nail Rubrics

113^c.9 | ARTIFICIAL NAIL SERVICE

Knowledge of the products, tools and services available for artificial nails allows you to add these services to your available repertoire. Combined with your knowledge of guest relations and plenty of practice, you will be able to provide professional artificial nail services that will leave your clients with a lasting impression that goes beyond being happy with the final result.

ARTIFICIAL NAIL CLIENT GUIDELINES

Now that you have a thorough understanding of artificial nail services, you are ready to apply your knowledge by performing safe and comfortable services with professional results.

These guidelines will help ensure your client's comfort and safety during a nail service.

	**PREPARE NAILS**	**Perform basic manicure without soaking nails and massaging hands:** » Check for client comfort while pushing the cuticles back. » Hold sidewalls while removing the shine to avoid filing on the client's skin. » Use caution, being careful not to touch the skin with dehydrator.
	**SIZE**	**Size and apply tips:** » Avoid using a tip that is too small; it may create fine cracks in the tip or it may "pinch" the client's fingernail, making their nails feel sensitive. » When using tip cutters the blade should face you and not client's finger.
	**APPLY**	**Apply product evenly and smoothly to save time balancing and finishing:** » Avoid getting product on the client's skin. » Check for client comfort to make sure there is no "burning" sensation.
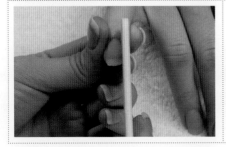	**BALANCE AND FINISH**	**File using long strokes and light pressure to avoid creating too much friction and causing a heat burn:** » Check client's comfort while filing. » Be sure to hold the sidewalls to avoid filing the client's skin.

ARTIFICIAL NAIL SERVICE OVERVIEW

The Artificial Nail Service Overview identifies the three areas of every artificial nail service:

» The Artificial Nail Preparation provides a brief overview of the steps to follow *before* you actually begin the nail service.

» The Artificial Nail Service Procedure provides an overview of the four steps that you will use *during* the nail service to ensure predictable results.

» The Artificial Nail Service Completion provides an overview of the steps to follow *after* performing the nail service to ensure guest satisfaction.

DISCOVERMORE

Practice Makes Perfect!

Experiment with different artificial nail products. Do some research with your mentors to find out which products they use and what worked for them when they were new to artificial nails. Did they prefer applying tips or performing sculptured nails? How did they perfect their smile lines when performing a two-color application? Take it all in and then... PRACTICE! Discover what you enjoy most and what works for you.

ARTIFICIAL NAIL SERVICE OVERVIEW

ARTIFICIAL NAIL SERVICE PREPARATION	» Clean and disinfect workstation. » Arrange disinfected tools, supplies and equipment. » Wash your hands. » Ask client to wash hands. » Perform an analysis of skin and nails. » Remove polish and perform a thorough visual analysis of the nails. » Consult with client about desired shape and/or length of nails.
ARTIFICIAL NAIL SERVICE PROCEDURE	» Perform artificial nail service procedures to achieve desired results: 1. **Prepare nails** by filing and shaping, performing cuticle care and removing the shine from the nails. 2. **Size** nail tips to match the C-curve of the nails, being careful not to cover more than half the nail (if applicable). 3. **Apply** nail product to a properly prepared nail, free of oils and debris. 4. **Balance and finish** using long strokes to avoid overheating the client's nails.
ARTIFICIAL NAIL SERVICE COMPLETION	» Reinforce client's satisfaction with overall salon experience. » Make professional product recommendations. » Prebook client's next appointment. » End client's visit with a warm and personal goodbye. » Discard single-use supplies; disinfect tools and multi-use supplies; disinfect workstation and arrange in proper order. » Complete client record.

ARTIFICIAL NAIL RUBRICS

A performance rubric is a document that identifies defined criteria at which levels of performance can be measured objectively.
Each Artificial Nail Rubric is an example that your instructor might choose to use for scoring. Each artificial nail service rubric is divided into three main areas—Preparation, Procedure and Completion. Each area is further divided into step-by-step procedures that will ensure client safety and satisfaction.

NAIL TIPS RUBRIC

Allotted Time: 20 Minutes

Student Name: _____ ID Number: _____

Instructor: _____ Date: _____ Start Time: _____ End Time: _____

NAIL TIPS (Live Model) – Each scoring item is marked with either a "Yes" or a "No." Each "Yes" counts for one point. Total number of points attainable is 31.

CRITERIA	YES	NO	INSTRUCTOR ASSESSMENT
PREPARATION: Did student...			
1. Set up workstation with properly labeled supplies?	☐	☐	
2. Place disinfected tools and supplies at a visibly clean workstation?	☐	☐	
3. Wash their hands?	☐	☐	
Connect: Did student...			
4. Meet and greet client with a welcoming smile and pleasant tone of voice?	☐	☐	
5. Communicate to build rapport and develop a relationship with client?	☐	☐	
6. Refer to client by name throughout service?	☐	☐	
Consult: Did student...			
7. Ask questions to discover client's wants and needs?	☐	☐	
8. Gain feedback and consent from client before proceeding?	☐	☐	
PROCEDURE: Did student...			
9. Ask client to wash hands and perform thorough visual analysis of skin and nails?	☐	☐	
10. Remove polish and analyze client's hands and nails and check for any contraindications?	☐	☐	
Create: Did student...			
11. Select the correct size nail tips for each finger?	☐	☐	
12. File and shape all nails to a rounded shape?	☐	☐	
13. Remove shine from the nails of each hand?	☐	☐	
14. Remove oil and debris from nail plates?	☐	☐	
15. Apply adhesive to tip of free edge of natural nail and to well of nail tip for all nails?	☐	☐	
16. Apply tip holding it at a slight angle, sliding toward free edge of natural nail until it is against the position stop?	☐	☐	
17. Repeat on all nails?	☐	☐	
18. Trim tips of all nails?	☐	☐	
19. Measure length to ensure consistency?	☐	☐	
20. Shape and blend tips using a 180-grit or higher file?	☐	☐	
21. Remove oils and debris from nail plates?	☐	☐	
22. Practice infection control procedures and safety guidelines throughout service?	☐	☐	
COMPLETION (Complete): Did student...			
23. Ask questions and look for verbal and nonverbal cues to determine client's level of satisfaction?	☐	☐	
24. Make professional product recommendations?	☐	☐	
25. Ask client to make a future appointment?	☐	☐	
26. End client's visit with a warm and personal goodbye?	☐	☐	
27. Discard single-use supplies?	☐	☐	
28. Disinfect tools and multi-use supplies; disinfect workstation and arrange in proper order?	☐	☐	
29. Complete service within scheduled time?	☐	☐	
30. Complete client record?	☐	☐	
31. Wash their hands following the service?	☐	☐	

COMMENTS: _____ TOTAL POINTS = _____ ÷ 31 = _____ %

ACRYLIC OVERLAY RUBRIC

Allotted Time: 45 Minutes

Student Name: _____ ID Number: _____

Instructor: _____ Date: _____ Start Time: _____ End Time: _____

ACRYLIC OVERLAY (Live Model) — Each scoring item is marked with either a "Yes" or a "No." Each "Yes" counts for one point. Total number of points attainable is 27.

CRITERIA	YES	NO	INSTRUCTOR ASSESSMENT
PREPARATION: Did student...			
1. Set up workstation with properly labeled supplies?	☐	☐	
2. Place disinfected tools and supplies at a visibly clean workstation?	☐	☐	
3. Wash their hands?	☐	☐	
Connect: Did student...			
4. Meet and greet client with a welcoming smile and pleasant tone of voice?	☐	☐	
5. Communicate to build rapport and develop a relationship with client?	☐	☐	
6. Refer to client by name throughout service?	☐	☐	
Consult: Did student...			
7. Ask questions to discover client's wants and needs?	☐	☐	
8. Gain feedback and consent from client before proceeding?	☐	☐	
PROCEDURE: Did student...			
9. Ask client to wash hands, analyze client's hands and check for any contraindications?	☐	☐	
Create: Did student...			
10. Prepare natural nails by filing, performing cuticle care and buffing as demonstrated in Basic Manicure Workshop?	☐	☐	
11. Apply tips (if desired)?	☐	☐	
12. Apply primer to all nails, if necessary?	☐	☐	
13. Prepare acrylic products?	☐	☐	
14. Apply acrylic at free edge (Zone 1), then middle of nail plate (Zone 2), and finally cuticle area (Zone 3)?	☐	☐	
15. Repeat acrylic application on all nails?	☐	☐	
16. File and shape nails?	☐	☐	
17. Buff nails and apply cuticle oil?	☐	☐	
18. Practice infection control procedures and safety guidelines throughout service?	☐	☐	
COMPLETION (Complete): Did student...			
19. Ask questions and look for verbal and nonverbal cues to determine client's level of satisfaction?	☐	☐	
20. Make professional product recommendations?	☐	☐	
21. Ask client to make a future appointment?	☐	☐	
22. End client's visit with a warm and personal goodbye?	☐	☐	
23. Discard single-use supplies?	☐	☐	
24. Disinfect tools and multi-use supplies; disinfect workstation and arrange in proper order?	☐	☐	
25. Complete service within scheduled time?	☐	☐	
26. Complete client record?	☐	☐	
27. Wash their hands following the service?	☐	☐	

COMMENTS: _____ TOTAL POINTS = _____ ÷ 27 = _____ %

PINK AND WHITE ACRYLIC SCULPTURED NAILS RUBRIC

Allotted Time: 1 Hour, 30 Minutes

Student Name: _____ ID Number: _____

Instructor: _____ Date: _____ Start Time: _____ End Time: _____

PINK AND WHITE ACRYLIC SCULPTURED NAILS (Live Model) — Each scoring item is marked with either a "Yes" or a "No." Each "Yes" counts for one point. Total number of points attainable is 28.

CRITERIA	YES	NO	INSTRUCTOR ASSESSMENT
PREPARATION: Did student...			
1. Set up workstation with properly labeled supplies?	☐	☐	
2. Place disinfected tools and supplies at a visibly clean workstation?	☐	☐	
3. Wash their hands?	☐	☐	
Connect: Did student...			
4. Meet and greet client with a welcoming smile and pleasant tone of voice?	☐	☐	
5. Communicate to build rapport and develop a relationship with client?	☐	☐	
6. Refer to client by name throughout service?	☐	☐	
Consult: Did student...			
7. Ask questions to discover client's wants and needs?	☐	☐	
8. Gain feedback and consent from client before proceeding?	☐	☐	
PROCEDURE: Did student...			
9. Ask client to wash hands, analyze client's hands and check for any contraindications?	☐	☐	
Create: Did student...			
10. Prepare natural nails by filing, performing cuticle care and buffing as demonstrated in Basic Manicure Workshop?	☐	☐	
11. Apply dehydrant (if necessary)?	☐	☐	
12. Apply nail forms to all nails?	☐	☐	
13. Prepare acrylic products?	☐	☐	
14. Apply white acrylic at free edge (Zone 1), then pink acrylic to middle of the nail plate (Zone 2), and finally, pink acrylic to cuticle area (Zone 3)?	☐	☐	
15. Repeat acrylic application on all nails?	☐	☐	
16. Remove forms from all nails?	☐	☐	
17. File and shape nails?	☐	☐	
18. Buff nails and apply cuticle oil?	☐	☐	
19. Practice infection control procedures and safety guidelines throughout service?	☐	☐	
COMPLETION (Complete): Did student...			
20. Ask questions and look for verbal and nonverbal cues to determine client's level of satisfaction?	☐	☐	
21. Make professional product recommendations?	☐	☐	
22. Ask client to make a future appointment?	☐	☐	
23. End client's visit with a warm and personal goodbye?	☐	☐	
24. Discard single-use supplies?	☐	☐	
25. Disinfect tools and multi-use supplies; disinfect workstation and arrange in proper order?	☐	☐	
26. Complete service within scheduled time?	☐	☐	
27. Complete client record?	☐	☐	
28. Wash their hands following the service?	☐	☐	

COMMENTS: _____

TOTAL POINTS = _____ ÷ 28 = _____ %

SALON**CONNECTION**

Knowledge = Trust

It is important to know the products and tools you are working with. Many clients know from personal experience or know someone who has had a bad experience with an artificial nail service. Gain your clients' trust by educating them on the products you are using and by answering all their questions. This will assure your clients that they have made the right decision to come to you!

LESSONS LEARNED

Procedural guidelines to follow when performing artificial nail services include:

» Prepare nails by performing a basic manicure (without soaking nails or massage) and ensure all oils and debris are removed from nail plates.

» Size nail tips to ensure a good fit without gaps (if applicable).

» Apply nail product to the nail to create a smooth, even finish that is thickest in Zone 2.

» Use long, slow strokes with the file to avoid overheating the client's nails while balancing and finishing.

» The three areas of artificial nail service include Preparation, Procedure and Completion.

  » Preparation includes setting up the workstation with disinfected tools and supplies and connecting with the client.

  » Procedure includes ensuring client safety and performing the artificial nail service.

  » Completion includes reinforcing client's level of satisfaction, recommending products, asking client to make a future appointment, disinfecting workstation and completing the client record.

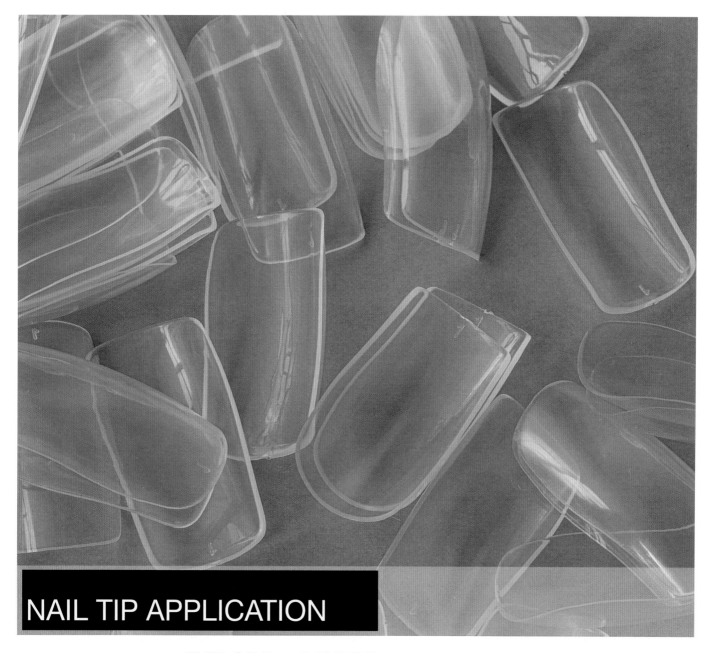

NAIL TIP APPLICATION

Nail tips come in a variety of shapes and even colors. What types of nail tips have you seen or worn?

INSPIRE

Nail tips are the foundation for acrylic and gel overlay services and can quickly add length and strength to your client's own nails.

ACHIEVE

Following this *Nail Tip Application Workshop*, you'll be able to:

» Apply tips and blend if necessary

PERFORMANCE GUIDE

NAIL TIP APPLICATION

View the video, then perform this workshop. Complete the
self-check as you progress through the workshop.

20 mins
Suggested
Salon Speed

PREPARATION ✔

» Assemble tools/implements/supplies and products
» Set up workstation
» Wash your hands
» Ask client to wash hands
» Perform analysis for signs of diseases or disorders

☐

---

1. **Remove nail polish and perform a thorough hand and nail visual analysis:**

» Consult with client about desired shape and length of nail tips

☐

NAIL PREPARATION – SIZE

2. **Select correct size of nail tips:**
» Match width of nail (sidewall to sidewall)
» Tip well covers no more than ⅓ to ½ of nail bed
» Bevel well of nail tip

☐

---

3. **File and shape nails of both hands:**

» Trim nails if necessary
» Round free edge of nails for tip application

☐

---

4. **Remove shine from nails of both hands:**
   » Lightly buff surface of nails using a 240-grit file

5. **Remove oils and debris from nail plates:**
   » Use lint-free nail wipe and nail preparation solution

APPLY

6. **Apply adhesive:**
   » Apply thin line of adhesive to free edge of natural nail and well of tip
   » Lightly press and drag the well of tip against nail toward free edge to spread adhesive evenly

7. **Apply tip to nail:**
   » Hold tip at slight angle, make contact with free edge and slide tip toward cuticle until free edge is against "position stop"
   » Rock tip down until it is flat against nail plate
   » Hold tip in place for a few seconds

8. **Repeat steps 6 and 7 on all fingernails.**

TRIM AND FILE

9. **Trim tips:**
   » Use tip cutters, blade toward you, or toenail clippers
   » Repeat on all nails

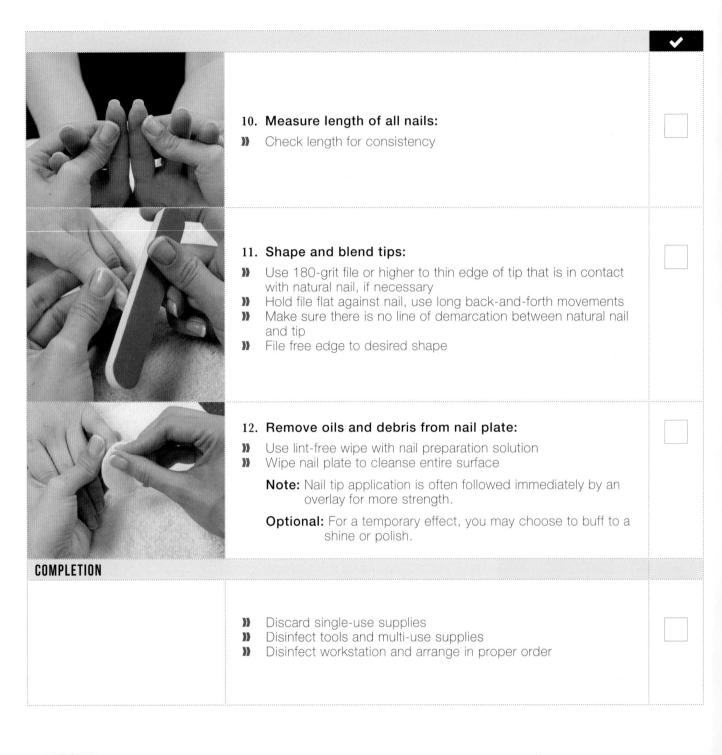

10. **Measure length of all nails:**
   » Check length for consistency

11. **Shape and blend tips:**
   » Use 180-grit file or higher to thin edge of tip that is in contact with natural nail, if necessary
   » Hold file flat against nail, use long back-and-forth movements
   » Make sure there is no line of demarcation between natural nail and tip
   » File free edge to desired shape

12. **Remove oils and debris from nail plate:**
   » Use lint-free wipe with nail preparation solution
   » Wipe nail plate to cleanse entire surface

   Note: Nail tip application is often followed immediately by an overlay for more strength.

   Optional: For a temporary effect, you may choose to buff to a shine or polish.

COMPLETION

   » Discard single-use supplies
   » Disinfect tools and multi-use supplies
   » Disinfect workstation and arrange in proper order

20 mins
Suggested Salon Speed

My Speed
_____
_____
_____

INSTRUCTIONS:
Record your time in comparison with the suggested salon speed. Then, list here how you could improve your performance.

_____
_____
_____
_____
_____

ACRYLIC OVERLAY

EXPLORE

Do you like wearing your nails with an acrylic overlay? If so, what do you like about it?

INSPIRE

A successful acrylic overlay service can make a client very loyal; they'll return for fill-ins and rebalancing.

ACHIEVE

Following this *Acrylic Overlay Workshop*, you'll be able to:

» Perform an acrylic overlay

PERFORMANCE GUIDE
ACRYLIC OVERLAY

View the video, then perform this workshop. Complete the
self-check as you progress through the workshop.

45
mins
Suggested
Salon Speed

PREPARATION ✔

» Assemble tools/implements/supplies and products » Set up workstation » Wash your hands » Ask client to wash their hands » Perform visual analysis for signs of diseases or disorders	☐

1. Remove nail polish and perform an analysis of the hands and nails: » Consult with client about desired shape and length of nails	☐

NAIL PREPARATION

2. Prepare natural nails by performing filling, cuticle care and buffing as demonstrated in the *Basic Manicure Workshop*.	☐

Optional: Apply tips as shown in the *Nail Tip Application Workshop*.	☐

3. **Apply primer, if necessary, to all nails:**

» Apply to natural nail
» Avoid touching the skin with primer
» Allow to dry
» Follow manufacturer's instructions

APPLY

4. **Prepare acrylic products:**

» Submerge the brush in monomer
» Wipe brush on side of dappen dish to flatten
» Form a bead on side or tip of acrylic brush

5. **Apply acrylic to at free edge (Zone 1):**

» Medium-size bead
» Pat and press from side to side following curve of nail
» Hold brush parallel to nail
» Product should be thinnest at free edge

6. **Apply acrylic to the middle of nail plate (Zone 2):**

» Medium-to-large size bead
» Pat and press following curve of nail
» Hold brush at approximately 45° angle
» Product should be thinnest at sidewalls
» Blend with Zone 1

7. **Apply acrylic to cuticle area (Zone 3):**

» Small-size bead
» Pat and press following the curve of the nail
» Hold brush at slightly higher angle than 45°
» Product should be thinnest at sidewalls and cuticle
» Blend with Zone 2

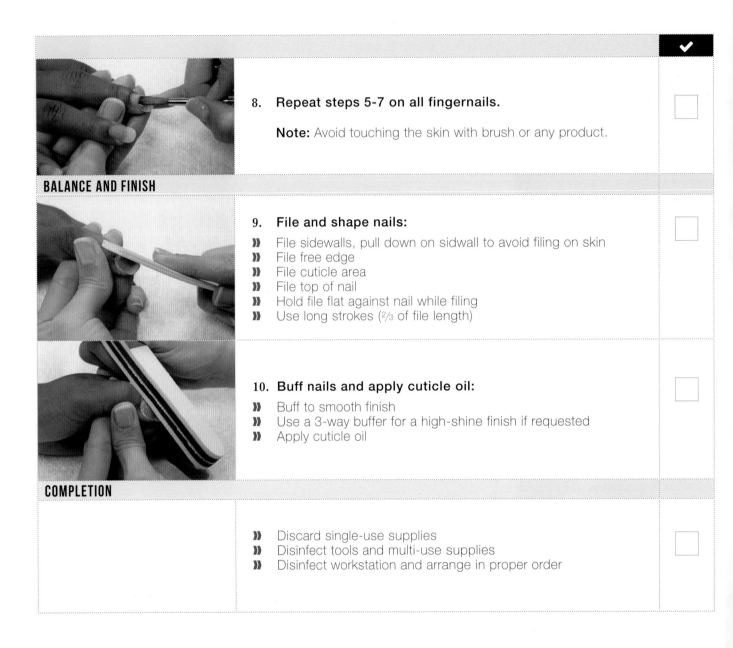

8. **Repeat steps 5-7 on all fingernails.**

   Note: Avoid touching the skin with brush or any product.

BALANCE AND FINISH

9. **File and shape nails:**
   » File sidewalls, pull down on sidwall to avoid filing on skin
   » File free edge
   » File cuticle area
   » File top of nail
   » Hold file flat against nail while filing
   » Use long strokes (²/₃ of file length)

10. **Buff nails and apply cuticle oil:**
    » Buff to smooth finish
    » Use a 3-way buffer for a high-shine finish if requested
    » Apply cuticle oil

COMPLETION

   » Discard single-use supplies
   » Disinfect tools and multi-use supplies
   » Disinfect workstation and arrange in proper order

45 mins
Suggested
Salon Speed

My Speed
_____
_____
_____

INSTRUCTIONS:
Record your time in comparison with the suggested salon speed. Then, list here how you could improve your performance.

_____
_____
_____
_____
_____

PINK AND WHITE
ACRYLIC SCULPTURED NAILS

EXPLORE

What differences do you notice between an artificial overlay and sculpted manicure?

INSPIRE

Beautifully sculpted nails in two colors showcase your skills and offers clients a natural-looking, long-lasting French manicure.

ACHIEVE

Following this *Pink and White Acrylic Sculptured Nails Workshop*, you'll be able to:

» Perform a two-color sculptured nail service.

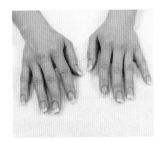

PERFORMANCE GUIDE

PINK AND WHITE ACRYLIC SCULPTURED NAILS

View the video, then perform this workshop. Complete the self-check as you progress through the workshop.

1 hr 30 mins
Suggested Salon Speed

PREPARATION ✓

» Assemble tools, supplies and products » Set up workstation » Wash your hands » Ask client to wash their hands » Perform visual analysis for signs of diseases or disorders	☐
1. Remove polish and perform a thorough visual analysis of the hands and nails: » Consult with client about desired shape and length of nails	☐

NAIL PREPARATION

2. Prepare natural nails by performing filing, cuticle care and buffing as demonstrated in the *Basic Manicure Workshop*.	☐
3. Apply dehydrant, if necessary, to all nails: » Apply to natural nail » Avoid touching skin » Allow to dry » Follow manufacturer's instructions	☐

4. **Apply nail forms:**
- » Slide nail form under client's nail
- » Do not force form
- » Make sure form fits snugly under edge, is positioned in a c-curve and is even with client's nail

5. **Apply primer, if necessary, to all nails:**
- » Apply to natural nail
- » Avoid touching skin
- » Allow to dry
- » Follow manufacturer's instructions

APPLY

6. **Prepare the acrylic products:**
- » Prepare powders in separate dappen dishes
- » Submerge brush in monomer
- » Wipe brush on side of dappen dish to flatten

7. **Apply acrylic at free edge (Zone 1):**
- » Medium size bead (white powder)
- » Pat and press from side to side following curve of nail
- » Hold brush parallel to nail
- » Product should be thinnest at free edge
- » Define smile line

8. **Apply acrylic to the middle of nail plate (Zone 2):**
- » Medium-to-large size bead (pink powder)
- » Pat and press following curve of nail to define shape and length of free edge
- » Hold brush at approximately 45° angle
- » Product should be thinnest at sidewalls
- » Blend with Zone 1

9. **Apply acrylic to cuticle area (Zone 3):**
   » Small size bead (pink powder)
   » Pat and press following curve of nail
   » Hold brush at slightly higher angle than 45°
   » Product should be thinnest at sidewalls and cuticle
   » Blend with Zone 2

10. **Repeat steps 8-10 on all fingers.**

    Note: Avoid touching the skin with the brush or any product.

11. **Remove forms:**
    » Make sure acrylic is dry
    » Carefully remove forms

BALANCE AND FINISH

12. **File and shape nails:**
    » File sidewalls, pull down on the sidewall to avoid filing on skin
    » File free edge
    » File cuticle area
    » File top of nail
    » Hold file flat against nail
    » Use long strokes (⅔ of file length)

13. **Repeat on all nails.**

14. **Buff nails and apply cuticle oil:**
   ➤ Buff to a smooth finish
   ➤ Use a 3-way buffer for a high shine finish if requested
   ➤ Apply cuticle oil

COMPLETION

➤ Discard single-use supplies
➤ Disinfect tools and multi-use supplies
➤ Disinfect workstation and arrange in proper order

1 hr 30 mins
Suggested Salon Speed

My Speed

INSTRUCTIONS:

Record your time in comparison with the suggested salon speed. Then, list here how you could improve your performance.

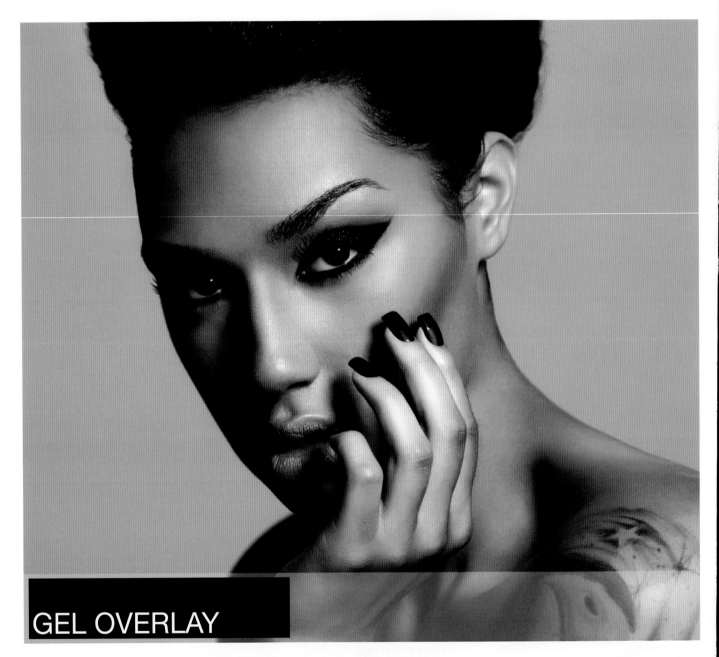

GEL OVERLAY

EXPLORE

Have you ever walked into a salon and been overwhelmed by acrylic nail fumes?

INSPIRE

Gel overlays are a great option for clients who want length added to their nails without using acrylic.

ACHIEVE

Following this *Gel Overlay Workshop*, you'll be able to:

» Perform a gel overlay

GEL OVERLAY

View the video, then perform this workshop. Complete the self-check as you progress through the workshop.

60 mins
Suggested Salon Speed

PREPARATION	✔

» Assemble tools/implements/supplies and products
» Set up workstation
» Wash your hands
» Ask client to wash their hands
» Perform visual analysis for signs of diseases or disorders

☐

1. **Remove nail polish and perform visual analysis of the hands and nails:**

» Consult with client about desired shape and length of nails

☐

NAIL PREPARATION	

2. **Prepare natural nails by performing filling, cuticle care and buffing as demonstrated in the *Basic Manicure Workshop*.**

☐

Optional: Apply tips as shown in the *Nail Tip Application Workshop*.

☐

3. **Apply gel primer, if necessary, to all nails:**

» Apply to natural nail
» Avoid touching the skin with primer
» Cure primer if necessary
» Follow manufacturer's instructions

☐

APPLY ✓

4. **Apply first layer of gel on little finger through index finger of first hand:**
   » Obtain small amount of gel using brush
   » Place gel on nail
   » Lightly brush into place
   » Apply base layer to entire nail, including free edge (Zone 1)

5. **Cure nails:**
   » Place fingers under light
   » Cure for manufacturer's recommended time
   » Avoid tilting fingers; keep them as level as possible

6. **Repeat steps 4 and 5 on second hand while first hand cures.**

7. **Repeat steps 4 and 5 to thumbs of both hands:**
   » Cure thumbs together

8. **Apply second layer of gel on little finger through index finger, first hand:**
   » Obtain small amount of gel using brush
   » Place gel in middle of nail plate
   » Blend gel into Zone 1
   » Apply to free edge to seal
   » Make sure product is thinnest at sidewalls

9. **Cure nails:**
   » Place fingers under light
   » Cure for manufactuer's recommended time
   » Avoid tilting fingers; keep them as level as possible

10. **Repeat steps 8 and 9 on second hand while first hand cures.**

11. Repeat steps 8 and 9 on thumbs of both hands:

» Cure thumbs together

12. Apply third layer of gel on little finger through index finger, first hand:

» Obtain small amount of gel using brush
» Place gel on nail
» Lightly brush into place to blend Zones 1, 2 and cuticle area (3)
» Apply coat of gel to entire nail
» Fill in any uneven areas if necessary

13. Cure nails:

» Place fingers under light
» Cure for manufacturer's recommended time
» Avoid tilting fingers; keep them as level as possible

14. Repeat steps 12 and 13 on second hand while first hand cures.

15. Repeat steps 12 and 13 on thumbs on both hands:

» Cure thumbs together

16. Remove sticky residue:

» Using manufacturer's recommended product, remove sticky residue from all nails

BALANCE AND FINISH ✔

17. File and shape nails:
- » File sidewalls, pull down on sidewall to avoid filing on skin
- » File free edge
- » File cuticle area
- » File top of nail
- » Hold flat against nail
- » Use long strokes (⅔ of file length)
- » Wipe nail plates using manufacturer's recommended product, remove debris from all nails

☐

18. Apply a finishing gel or sealer gel little finger through index finger, first hand:
- » Apply product to free edge to seal
- » Cure for recommended time

☐

19. Repeat step 18 on second hand while the first hand cures.

☐

20. Repeat step 18 on the thumbs of both hands.

☐

21. Remove sticky residue:
- » Using manufacturer's recommended product, remove sticky residue from all nails
- » Polish if desired

☐

COMPLETION

- » Discard single-use supplies
- » Disinfect tools and multi-use supplies
- » Disinfect workstation and arrange in proper order

☐

60 mins Suggested Salon Speed

My Speed
_____
_____
_____

INSTRUCTIONS:
Record your time in comparison with the suggested salon speed. Then, list here how you could improve your performance.

_____
_____
_____
_____

113ᶜ GLOSSARY/INDEX

Acrylic Nails *74*
Type of artificial nail enhancement created by using a combination of an acrylic powder and an acrylic liquid.

Acrylic Primer *75*
Product that ensures adhesion of acrylic product to nail.

Adhesive *78*
A tacky (sticky) substance that bonds a plastic tip to a natural nail; specially formulated for the nail industry.

Agnail (Hangnail) *14*
Split cuticle; loose skin partially separated from the cuticle.

Antiseptic *31*
Liquid or foam-based product used to reduce microbes on the skin.

Artificial Nails *74*
Use of various materials and techniques to strengthen and lengthen weak nails; conceal or repair chipped or broken nails.

Base Coat *32*
Colorless polish that evens out the nail plate, holds nail color to nail, prevents pigments from penetrating the nail plate.

Block Buffer *35*
Used to smooth surface of the nail.

Blue Nails *12*
Blue color in skin under nails; caused by systemic problems of the heart, poor circulation or injury.

Bruised Nail *14*
Nail condition identified by dark, purplish discoloration under the nail; caused by trauma to nail, environmental problem, blood trapped under nails or hemorrhage of small capillaries.

Cleaning *44, 45*
Process of removing dirt and debris to aid in preventing the growth of microbes.

Corrugation *12*
Horizontal wavy ridges across the nail; caused by injury, systemic conditions.

Cuticle *6*
Overlapping dead tissue that is loose and pliable around the nail.

Cuticle Cream or Oil *32*
Moisturizer used to soften cuticle skin; moisturizes brittle nails.

Cuticle Nipper *34*
Cutting implement used to trim hangnails.

Cuticle Pusher *34*
Implement used to loosen and push back cuticles.

Cuticle Remover Cream *31*
Low-percent hydrogen peroxide, sodium or potassium hydroxide used to loosen dead skin.

Dappen Dish *76*
Small glass container that holds monomer and polymer separately during nail service.

Dehydrant or Dehydrating Solution *32*
Solution that allows better adhesion of nail enhancements; reduces the amount of moisture in the nail when brushed over the nail plate.

Disinfection *44, 45, 46*
Infection control method that kills certain but not all microbes.

Effleurage *25*
Light, gliding massage strokes or circular motions made with the palms of the hands or pads of the fingertips; often used to begin and/or end a treatment; often used on the face, neck and arms because of its gentleness.

Eggshell Nails *12*
Very thin, soft nails.

Emery Board *34*
Implement used to shorten and shape natural nails.

Eponychium *6*
Live tissue at the base of the nail.

Etiology *8*
Cause of a disease, disorder or condition.

Exfoliant *33*
Granular scrub or sloughing lotion that removes dead skin cells.

Free Edge *6*
Part of the nail that extends beyond the end of the finger or toe and protects the tips of the fingers and toes.

French Manicure *27*
Nail polishing technique/design to create a natural-looking effect; white polish is applied to the free edge of the nail and a sheer pink or beige polish applied to the entire nail plate.

Friction *25*
Stimulating circular or wringing massage movement with no gliding; increases circulation; performed with the fingertips or palms of the hands, rather than moving across the skin, the skin moves either across the muscle or the bone beneath it.

Furrow *13*
Indented vertical line down the nail plate.

Gel Bonder *77*
Gel primer; thin gel or liquid that ensures adhesion of gel product to nail.

Gel or Light-Cured Nails *77*
Nail enhancements created using a gel-like product containing acrylic oligomers; uses a light source to harden the product.

Gel Sealer *77*
Thin gel product that creates a high-shine finish and seals product.

Hyponychium *6*
Living tissue underneath the free edge of the nail.

Pedicure   *22*
Cosmetic care of the feet and toenails; the Latin word "ped" means foot and "cura" means care.

Pedicure Basin/Bath   *38*
A container that allows comfortable soaking of feet for a pedicure service.

Perionychium   *6*
The living tissue that overlies the nail plate on the sides of the nail.

Petrissage   *25*
Light or heavy kneading and rolling of the muscles; performed by kneading muscles between the thumb and fingers or by pressing the palm of the hand firmly over the muscles, then grasping and squeezing with the heel of the hand and fingers; generally performed from the front of the head to the back; used on the face, arms, shoulders and upper back.

Polymer   *75*
Nail product that is mixed with a monomer to form an acrylic nail; powder in form.

Pterygium   *14*
Living skin attached to nail plate either at the eponychium (dorsal pterygium) or hyponychium (inverse pterygium).

Sculptured Nails   *81*
Nail enhancement created over a nail form, rather than using a tip for added length.

Sidewalls   *6*
Folds of skin on either side of the nail groove.

Sloughing Lotion   *33*
Exfoliating product that removes dead skin cells.

Speed Dry   *33*
Drying agent; spray or polish which aids in fast drying of polish.

Tapotement or Percussion   *25*
Light tapping or slapping massage movement; performed with fingertips or partly flexed fingers.

Tinea Manus   *10*
Ringworm of the hand.

Tinea Pedis   *10*
Athlete's foot or ringworm of the feet.

Tinea Unguium or Unguis   *10*
Ringworm of the nail.

Top Coat or Sealer   *33*
Colorless, clear polish that dries to a high shine; protects colored polish from chipping, fading and peeling.

Viscosity   *77*
Thickness of a product; high viscosity means thicker; low viscosity means thinner.

PIVOT POINT

 ACKNOWLEDGMENTS

Pivot Point Fundamentals is designed to provide education to undergraduate students to help prepare them for licensure and an entry-level position in the cosmetology field. An undertaking of this magnitude requires the expertise and cooperation of many people who are experts in their field. Pivot Point takes pride in our internal team of educators who develop cosmetology, esthetics and nails education, along with our print and digital experts, designers, editors, illustrators and video producers. Pivot Point would like to express our many thanks to these talented individuals who have devoted themselves to the business of beauty, lifelong learning and especially for help raising the bar for future professionals in our industry.

EDUCATION DEVELOPMENT	**Janet Fisher // Sabine Held-Perez // Vasiliki A. Stavrakis**
	Markel Artwell
	Eileen Dubelbeis
	Brian Fallon
	Melissa Holmes
	Lisa Luppino
	Paul Suttles
	Amy Gallagher
	Lisa Kersting
	Jamie Nabielec
	Vic Piccolotto
	Ericka Thelin
	Jane Wegner
EDITORIAL	**Maureen Spurr // Wm. Bullion // Deidre Glover**
	Liz Bagby
	Jack Bernin
	Lori Chapman
DESIGN & PRODUCTION	**Jennifer Eckstein // Rick Russell // Danya Shaikh**
	Joanna Jakubowicz
	Denise Podlin
	Annette Baase
	Agnieszka Hansen
	Kristine Palmer
	Tiffany Wu
PROJECT MANAGEMENT	**Jenny Allen // Ken Wegrzyn**
DIGITAL DEVELOPMENT	John Bernin
	Javed Fouch
	Anna Fehr
	Matt McCarthy
	Marcia Noriega
	Corey Passage
	Herb Potzus

Pivot Point also wishes to take this opportunity to acknowledge the many contributors and product concept testers who helped make this program possible.

INDUSTRY CONTRIBUTORS

Linda Burmeister
Esthetics

Jeanne Braa Foster
Dr. Dean Foster
Eyes on Cancer

Mandy Gross
Nails

Andrea D. Kelly, MA, MSW
University of Delaware

Rosanne Kinley
Infection Control
National Interstate Council

Lynn Maestro
Cirépil by Perron Rigot, Paris

Andrzej Matracki
World and European
Men's Champion

MODERN SALON

Rachel Molepske
Look Good Feel Better, PBA
CUT IT OUT, PBA

Peggy Moon
Liaison to Regulatory and Testing

Robert Richards
Fashion Illustrations

Clif St. Germain, Ph.D
Educational Consultant

Andis Company

International Dermal Institute

HairUWear Inc.

Lock & Loaded Men's Grooming

PRODUCT CONCEPT TESTING

Central Carolina Community College
Millington, North Carolina

Gateway Community Colleges
Phoenix, Arizona

MC College
Edmonton, Alberta

Metro Beauty Academy
Allentown, Pennsylvania

Rowan Cabarrus Community College
Kannapolis, North Carolina

Sunstate Academy of Cosmetology and Massage
Ft. Myers, Florida

Summit Salon Academy
Kokomo, Indiana

TONI&GUY Hairdressing Academy
Costa Mesa, California
Plano, Texas

Xenon Academy
Omaha, NE
Grand Island, NE

LEADERSHIP TEAM

Robert Passage
Chairman and CEO

Robert J. Sieh
Senior Vice President,
Finance and Operations

Judy Rambert
Vice President, Education

Kevin Cameron
Senior Vice President,
Education and Marketing

R.W. Miller
Vice President, Domestic Sales
and Field Education

Jan Laan
Vice President, International
Business Development

Katy O'Mahony
Director, Human Resources

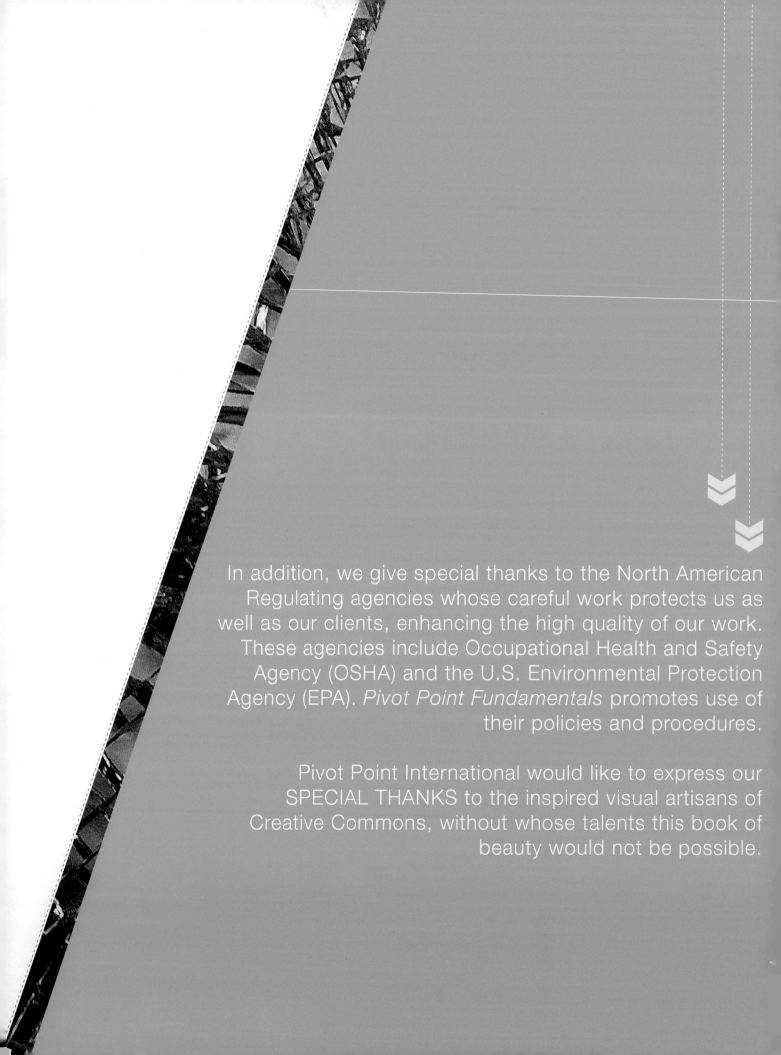

In addition, we give special thanks to the North American Regulating agencies whose careful work protects us as well as our clients, enhancing the high quality of our work. These agencies include Occupational Health and Safety Agency (OSHA) and the U.S. Environmental Protection Agency (EPA). *Pivot Point Fundamentals* promotes use of their policies and procedures.

Pivot Point International would like to express our SPECIAL THANKS to the inspired visual artisans of Creative Commons, without whose talents this book of beauty would not be possible.